CHURCHES
IN THE SHAPE OF
SCRIPTURE

CHURCHES OF CHRIST AND THE QUEST TO BE
MORE THAN JUST ANOTHER EVANGELICAL CHURCH

DAN CHAMBERS

Churches in the Shape of Scripture

Published by FaithWorks Press
2101 Georgian Circle
Franklin, Tennessee 37067

ISBN: 978-0-9858903-0-8

Design and layout: D.J. Smith, Talstone Group, Nashville, TN

Printed in the United States of America

DEDICATED

To all the good men
who have helped me understand
that theology and truth still matter.

CONTENTS

Preface

Chapter 1
NEW TESTAMENT-SHAPED CHURCHES
11

Chapter 2
SALVATION & CHURCH MEMBERSHIP
IN THE SHAPE OF THE NEW TESTAMENT
35

Chapter 3
MUSICAL PRAISE IN THE ASSEMBLY
IN THE SHAPE OF THE NEW TESTAMENT
67

Chapter 4
THE LORD'S DAY & THE LORD'S SUPPER
IN THE SHAPE OF THE NEW TESTAMENT
93

Chapter 5
GENDER ROLES IN THE ASSEMBLY
IN THE SHAPE OF THE NEW TESTAMENT
123

Chapter 6
CHURCH ORGANIZATION & LEADERSHIP
IN THE SHAPE OF THE NEW TESTAMENT
153

Chapter 7
MYTHS & MISCONCEPTIONS
ABOUT CHURCHES OF CHRIST
181

Endnotes
203

PREFACE

It's no secret that doctrine has been downplayed in American church life for some time now. In far too many places, deep teaching on the great doctrines of Scripture is a thing of the past, and almost no attention is given to how doctrine must govern the life of the local church.

It should come as no surprise then to find out that more and more professing Christians view the fundamentals of Christianity as little more than: (1) having some kind of belief that Jesus saves and (2) doing nice things for others—like generously tipping your waiter, making an occasional donation to your local church or charity of your choice, recycling and going green whenever possible, and for the most part trying to follow that do-unto-others rule.

For many modern churchgoers, all that really matters in a church is that it's warm and welcoming, has a service that brings them pleasure and moves them emotionally, and is making an impact for good in the community. For them, if a local church passes those three tests, the "religious brand" of that church—as well as its doctrine—is largely irrelevant.

We in churches of Christ haven't been immune to these cultural influences. When it comes to the historic doctrinal emphases of churches of Christ, there are plenty among us who no longer believe those things really matter. As a result, they wouldn't think twice about ditching our fellowship for a church group that's very different doctrinally.

I, however, believe doctrine still matters. I worship where I do, first and foremost, because of doctrine. For me, when it comes to choosing a church home, if the doctrine isn't right, no other consideration is relevant. Only when I believe a church's doctrine is right do I move on to ask things like: "Is this congregation warm and welcoming?"; "Are their worship assemblies generally uplifting and edifying?"; and "Are they making an impact for good in their community and around the world?"

A few years ago, Dr. Albert Mohler, the president of The Southern Baptist Theological Seminary, wrote, "We are reaping the harvest of doctrinal neglect. The urgency of this task cannot be ignored. Baptists will either recover our denominational heritage and rebuild our doctrinal foundations, or in the next generation there will be no authentic Baptist witness."

When I first read that statement my initial reaction was, "Wow, by changing just three words, that sentiment perfectly expresses my own feelings concerning churches of Christ." Here are those feelings (with my changes in italics): We are reaping the harvest of doctrinal neglect. The urgency of this task cannot be ignored. *Churches of Christ* will either recover our *restoration* heritage and rebuild our doctrinal foundations, or in the next generation there will be no authentic *restoration* witness.

This book is an attempt to do just that—help us recover our restoration heritage and rebuild our doctrinal foundations. I realize, of course, not every congregation needs to recover that heritage or rebuild those doctrinal foundations. For those congregations, hopefully this can be a useful resource to simply strengthen that heritage and those doctrinal foundations.

My ultimate prayer is that many will walk away from

this book with a renewed conviction that doing things God's way really matters, and a renewed commitment to take seriously every facet of the New Testament's teaching concerning the local church.

CHAPTER 1

NEW TESTAMENT-SHAPED CHURCHES

I picked up the phone and took the transferred call with my usual, somewhat terse, "This is Dan." On the other end, a pleasant female voice responded with her own introduction and a brief explanation of why she was calling our church office. She said she was new to our area, was looking for a church home, had noticed our building while driving around town, but had to admit that she really wasn't familiar with churches of Christ. Then she got down to business: "Could you tell me something about the church of Christ?"

"Sure," I replied, "I'd be glad to." But before I could launch into my "who-we-are" speech, she tossed this follow-up question at me: "Could you tell me what the difference is between the church of Christ and the _____ church?" and she named a very large, very prominent denomination. What followed was a twenty minute or so conversation in which I tried to give her a glimpse of what churches of Christ are all about and how we differ from other church groups.

She wasn't the first person to ask me about churches of Christ, and I know she won't be the last; and, in case you're wondering, I *never* get tired of answering people's questions about my church family. More than anything, and most importantly, I love to tell people about Jesus and what He did for them on the cross. But I also love to tell others about what we in churches of Christ are trying to be and do as His followers, and that's exactly what I want to do in this book—I want to tell you about churches of Christ.

Before I get rolling, though, let me make it very clear that I'm not presuming to speak for every member of every church of Christ, nor am I presuming to speak for every congregation that calls itself a church of Christ. I want to emphasize that for a couple of reasons. First, since churches of Christ aren't actually a denomination, nor do we want to be (I'll tell you more about that later), nobody can represent the beliefs and practices of churches of Christ in any "official" sense. Second, when it comes to the beliefs and practices of churches of Christ, the simple fact of the matter is, there's probably more diversity these days than ever. I can assure you there are plenty of members of churches of Christ who won't be buying this book as a stocking stuffer for friends and family next Christmas. And with equal assurance I can say there are plenty of churches of Christ that won't be using this book in their teen or adult education programs . . . *ever.*

Despite this diversity, however, I'm convinced there's still a general unity among churches of Christ when it comes to their basic convictions. In other words, I think the majority of churches of Christ are still committed to the same basic package of beliefs and practices. It's that majority, and that same package of beliefs and practices, which I'll be describing in this book. So, if I say "we" or "us" to refer to churches of Christ, keep in mind that I really mean *"most of us* in *most* churches of Christ."

With that out of the way, I'm now ready to get down to the business of helping you understand churches of Christ a little better . . . maybe even a lot better.

NOT JUST ANOTHER EVANGELICAL CHURCH

While flying home from Israel a couple of summers ago, my wife, Leola, and I found ourselves seated next to a really nice, and really talkative, twenty-something. He had the window seat, I was on the aisle, and Leola was sandwiched between us. While I was lost in a loaner book from my brother on the history of Major League Baseball, Leola and our new friend were getting to know each other.

I don't have a clue what they talked about most of the time, but I do know at some point the subject turned to the kind of church group we were traveling with because Leola woke me from my baseball-concentration coma with an elbow and a "Hey," and then asked, "Are we an evangelical church?"

When people who aren't familiar with churches of Christ are trying to get a handle on who we are, that's one of the first questions many of them ask: "Are churches of Christ evangelical churches?" So why don't we start with that question. Before I can answer it, though, I need to make sure we're on the same page when it comes to understanding what most people mean when they refer to evangelical churches. After all, even Leola wasn't quite sure what one was. In her defense, though, you just don't hear the word "evangelical" a whole lot among churches of Christ.

Over the last several years the word "evangelical" has become a little more slippery and therefore a little tougher to get a good grip on. I still think, however, when most people use the word "evangelical" to describe a church, they have in mind a church that's rock solid in its commitment to a few basic beliefs, one of which is that the Bible is literally God's book.

While evangelicals know it was red-blooded human beings who actually dipped their quills into the ink and put the words on the original pages of the sixty-six "books" of the Bible, they're also convinced God Himself supervised the writing in such a way that makes Him the actual author of every word of Scripture.

Another belief most evangelicals are tenaciously committed to is the belief that salvation can be received only through faith in Jesus Christ. In other words, evangelical churches teach that putting one's faith in Jesus isn't merely *a way* to eternal life, but rather it's *the only way.*

Finally, most evangelicals are equally unwavering in their belief that a person's life must change when he or she becomes a Christian. More specifically, they believe every Christian has an obligation to shape his or her thinking and behavior according to the will of God which is found in the Bible.

Now that we're on the same page in understanding what an evangelical church is, let's go back to the original question: "Are churches of Christ evangelical churches?" Based on my description, it's fair to say that most people would put us in that category. After all, most of us in churches of Christ are diehard in our belief that God is the ultimate author of the Bible. We're convinced beyond a shadow of a doubt that the Holy Spirit in some way supervised the writers of the Bible so that the words

they originally wrote were the exact words God wanted written
(2 Timothy 3:16-17; 2 Peter 1:21).

We're equally diehard in our belief that Jesus is the only way
to eternal life. We don't believe there's the slightest bit of wiggle-
room in Jesus's statement, "I am the way, and the truth, and the
life; no one comes to the Father but through Me" (John 14:6). Of
course, in a culture where diversity seems increasingly cham-
pioned above almost everything else, we realize this one-way
message doesn't endear us to our more politically correct friends
and neighbors. Nevertheless, we embrace this one-way message
without reluctance or apology.

Finally, we in churches of Christ are just as passionate in our
belief that Christians must live transformed lives. It's not exactly
breaking news that a lot of folks want God in their lives, but
they're not really interested in changing their lifestyles. Nor is
it breaking news that plenty of churches seem to offer salvation
without total moral transformation.

We, however, reject the notion of salvation without transformation with every ounce of our being. When God calls His people to
change how they live—that is, to repent—we believe it's a non-nego-
tiable command, not a recommendation we're free to opt out of if the
idea of being transformed doesn't really make our heart race
(Colossians 3:5-10; 1 Peter 1:14-16).

Now back to the airplane for the rest of the story. Even though
most of us in churches of Christ tend to shy away from putting
ourselves into categories (that's one reason you don't hear the
word "evangelical" used that much among us), I knew exactly

what the young man was looking for. He just wanted to know if we were one of those churches that believe the Bible is literally God's Word and that Jesus Christ is the only way to be saved. So, I leaned forward to by-pass Leola, smiled at our new friend, and said, "We sure are."

Even though, in most people's minds, our basic convictions put us squarely in the category of evangelical churches, and even though I usually don't hesitate to say "Yes" when someone asks if we're evangelical, I want you to know that we don't consider ourselves to be just another evangelical church. We believe there are some pretty significant differences between us and most other evangelical church groups, and you're about to find out what some of those differences are. First, though, let me tell you what being different doesn't mean.

DIFFERENT DOESN'T MEAN . . .

When I say we in churches of Christ are different than other church groups, it doesn't mean we think we're more zealous or more passionate about serving God than others. We don't believe that for a minute.

And when I say we're different, it doesn't mean we believe we're more sincere, more devoted, or more dedicated in our quest to obey God than others. We don't believe that for a minute either.

Nor does being different mean that we have more respect for the Bible as God's Word, or have purer motives, or are more Christ-like in our thinking and behavior than those in other church groups. We know none of those things are true.

So what do I mean when I say churches of Christ are different than other church groups? The difference begins with a radical idea.

THE RADICAL GOAL OF RESTORATION

I think I can say with a good bit of confidence that most churchgoers have heard of the religious movement which swept through Europe in the 1500s called the Reformation (or Protestant Reformation or Great Reformation). They may not know a whole lot about it, but at least they've heard of it.

I also feel pretty sure that most churchgoers have heard of the man usually credited with starting the Reformation, Martin Luther. Like the Reformation itself, they may not know much about Martin Luther, but at least they've heard of him.

The term "reformation" is used to describe this movement because the goal of men like Luther was to *reform* the morally and doctrinally corrupt Catholic establishment of their day. When Luther strolled up to the Castle Church door in Wittenberg, Germany on October 31, 1517 with a mallet, a nail, and a document known as his "ninety-five theses," unbeknownst to him, it was game-on for the Reformation, and the world would never be the same.

Martin Luther just happens to be one of my personal heroes, and I praise God for him and others like him who put their lives on the line to get the quest for spiritual truth moving in the right direction with their radical ideas of reform. But while the Reformation was definitely a huge step in the right direction, most of us in churches of Christ believe it fell just a little short in terms of the ultimate goal. As a result, we take the idea of reformation a step further. We embrace the idea of *restoration*. We claim to be part of a *restoration movement*.

We use the term "restoration" to describe this movement because our goal is to actually *restore* the true church of Jesus Christ in our day by *restoring* the beliefs and practices of the church in the New Testament. You can hear our passion for this goal when you hear some of us occasionally refer to ourselves as "New Testament churches." For instance, I might ask a fellow member, "Is there a New Testament church in that town?" or I might ask him, "How many New Testament churches are in such-and-such county (or city, or state, or country)?"

From time to time I hear people encourage others who are looking for a church home to find a "Bible-believing church." In other words, find a church that believes the Bible is literally God's communication to man, and is the ultimate authority for life.

As you've already seen, most churches of Christ are definitely Bible-believing churches. But most of us aren't satisfied with just being Bible-*believing* churches. We're just as passionate about being Bible-*shaped* churches. More specifically, we're trying very hard to be *New Testament-shaped* churches. Every noticeable difference between churches of Christ and other church groups springs from this radical goal of restoring Jesus's true church by restoring the beliefs and practices of His church in New Testament times.

WHY THE GOAL OF RESTORATION?

Why are we so intensely committed to this goal? First and

foremost, it's because we believe *restoration* is an idea that's strongly endorsed in the Bible. Let me explain and then show you what I mean. We'll start with what I believe are a few indisputable facts, and I think most Bible-believers will agree.

For one thing, it's an indisputable fact that the God of the Bible has always given His people instructions for life. Whether we're talking about His Old Testament people, Israel, or His New Testament people, the church, God has always instructed them in matters like how they're to be organized and governed, how they're to approach and worship Him, and how they're to morally and ethically live.

It's also an indisputable fact that God has always demanded complete obedience from His people. He repeatedly pounded into the heads of His Old Testament people the need to be fully obedient (Leviticus 26:14ff; Deuteronomy 30:15-20; Ecclesiastes 12:13-14; Isaiah 42:24-25), and He pounds the need for obedience into the heads of us New Testament believers as well (Matthew 7:21-27; Luke 6:46-49; John 14:21-24; 1 Corinthians 14:37-38).

Still another indisputable fact is that people don't always obey God. While some are defiant in their disobedience, the fact is, sometimes the will of God on a particular matter simply gets "lost," and as a result people just fail to carry out the true will of God. This is where the concept of *restoration* enters the picture.

When a doctrine of God is lost, most of us in churches of Christ are convinced that God wants that doctrine *restored.* In other words, He wants His people to once again start doing what He originally told them to do. Now let me show you a couple of examples in the Bible that I think teach the importance of *restoring* God's original commands if they're ever lost. If you've got a copy of the Old Testament handy, you may want to take a look at these stories for yourself after I give you the thumbnail sketch.

You'll find the first example in Nehemiah 8, and I'll quickly set the stage. The world of the Israelites fell apart in 586 B.C. when the Babylonian war-machine rolled into Jerusalem and leveled the place. Of course it was God who orchestrated the whole thing because Israel stubbornly refused to trust Him and live in obedience to His will. Most of those who were "lucky" enough to survive the Babylonian blitzkrieg were marched back to Babylon where they lived under the thumb of their conquerors for the next seventy years or so.

In Nehemiah 8 the nightmare of this captivity is finally over. Thanks to the Persians, the Babylonians became a footnote in history almost overnight. Suddenly, with a new superpower on the block, God's people were allowed to return to their homeland to resurrect their beloved Jerusalem and rebuild the temple of God.

The most exciting thing of all, however, is that a spirit of revival was sweeping over the land and people were flocking to Jerusalem hungry for God's Word. That spiritual hunger is on full display in this chapter as Ezra is publically reading the Law of Moses (Nehemiah 8:1), and the people are hanging on every word . . . for *hours* (Nehemiah 8:3). Now let's pick up the story on day two of this public Bible reading marathon (Nehemiah 8:13).

While Ezra is reading, something incredible happens. A discovery is made. It's discovered that God had commanded His

NEW TESTAMENT-SHAPED CHURCHES – CHAPTER 1

people to live in temporary booths, or huts, made out of tree branches during the seven-day Jewish festival known as the Feast of Tabernacles (Nehemiah 8:14).[1] A few verses later we're told that no one had been doing this "from the days of Joshua the son of Nun to that day" (Nehemiah 8:17).

Exactly how long had that been? Would you believe almost a thousand years? Imagine that—God's people had not been carrying out His living-in-huts command for almost ten centuries! Now *that* is a lost doctrine.

Then what? What was their response to this discovery? Hard as it may be to believe for us modern worshipers, apparently no one said, "Look, this isn't that big of a deal. We're still observing the Feast of Tabernacles and that's all that matters. If this hut-stuff were really important, don't you think people would have been doing it for the last thousand years? The fact that nobody's been doing it for a thousand years ought to tell us something, like quit sweating these minor details." And apparently nobody said, "Listen, before we rush into this hut-building-thing, I think we need to ask ourselves, 'Is this really a salvation issue?'" And apparently no one chimed in with this: "Hey, let's not get all legalistic about this."

These people were so committed to obeying God that they looked at each other and said, in effect, "Wow, that's enough Bible study for today. We're supposed to be sitting around in little huts while observing this feast. Let's go gather some sticks and get these huts built." Here are the actual words which describe their reaction to this discovery:

> So they proclaimed and circulated a proclamation in all
> their cities and in Jerusalem, saying, "Go out to the hills,
> and bring olive branches and wild olive branches, myrtle
> branches, palm branches and branches of other leafy trees,
> to make booths, as it is written." So the people went out
> and brought them and made booths for themselves, each
> on his roof, and in their courts and in the courts of the
> house of God, and in the square at the Water Gate and
> in the square at the Gate of Ephraim. The entire assem-
> bly of those who had returned from the captivity made
> booths and lived in them. The sons of Israel had indeed
> not done so from the days of Joshua the son of Nun to that
> day. And there was great rejoicing (Nehemiah 8:15-17).

That's a great example of *restoration* in living color. After discover-
ing a command of God that had been lost for almost a thousand years,
they *restored* it to its original place among the religious practices of
the community.

Another classic example of *restoration* took place about 550
years before the living-in-huts discovery in Nehemiah's day.
You'll find this one in 2 Samuel 6, and playing the lead role in
this drama is none other than the man after God's own heart himself, King David.

David hadn't been wearing the crown long when he started
thinking about the ark of the covenant. You see, years earlier, way
back in 1 Samuel 4, it was carted off by Israel's archnemesis, the
Philistines, as part of the spoils of victory after they had given
the Israelites a beat down on the battlefield. After holding onto
the ark for about seven months—seven very long, very miserable
months during which time they stayed on the business end of
God's wrath—the Philistines shipped it back to Israel where it

essentially remained in storage collecting dust for the next few decades. Then came David's coronation.

Unlike his predecessor Saul, David was on fire for the Lord, and he was determined to make his new capital city, Jerusalem, the center of worship for the kingdom. If that was going to happen, though, he knew he needed to get that piece of sacred furniture back in its rightful place in the tabernacle. After all, the glory of God rested upon that gold-covered chest. And that brings us to 2 Samuel 6—moving day for the ark of the covenant.

For David, when it came time to move the ark to Jerusalem, two men and a truck just wouldn't do. Since it represented the presence of God, moving it had to be a national event and all stops had to be pulled out. Step one was to assemble a 30,000 man honor guard and protection force to escort it the seven or so miles from storage to Jerusalem (2 Samuel 6:1). Step two included putting together musicians for the royal procession and celebration (2 Samuel 6:5). And then, of course, there was the incredibly important matter of how the ark would actually be transported.

I'm guessing there was quite a bit of discussion and deliberation over this matter of how to move the ark, and the text informs us that they settled on using a brand spanking new cart. I don't know about you, but that impresses me. They obviously put thought into this move, and what an incredible gesture of respect and reverence they came up with. This was the ark of the living God, so putting it on a used cart was simply out of the question (2 Samuel 6:3).

When the big day rolled around, things started off without a hitch. The ark was loaded on the shiny new cart, the musicians started doing their thing, and "all the house of Israel were celebrating before the Lord" (2 Samuel 6:5). For a little while, things chugged along according to plan. Soon, however, the plan was blown to smithereens by one of the most shocking moments you'll find anywhere in the Bible.

When the cart rolled over a rocky, rough threshing floor at a place called Nacon, it started bouncing around, and something unthinkable began to happen—the ark of the covenant was on the verge of tumbling off the cart. Luckily, though, there just happened to be a quick thinker by the name of Uzzah who was helping lead the cart, and he did what anyone in his right mind would have done. He reached out and grabbed it to keep it from hitting the ground. That *is* what anyone in his right mind would have done, right? I mean, who's going to just stand by and watch the ark of God slide off the tailgate? In most people's book Uzzah would have been a hero. If it were up to most people, his picture would have been on the front page of Jerusalem's newspaper the next morning under a headline that went something like, "Quick Thinking Uzzah Saves the Ark of the Covenant."

But that's not even close to what happened. Uzzah made the paper alright, but it wasn't the front page; it was closer to the back, in the obituaries. What happened was "the anger of the Lord burned against Uzzah, and God struck him down there for his irreverence and he died there by the ark of God" (2 Samuel 6:7). With a corpse at his feet, David suddenly got very angry and very scared—I'm thinking more scared than angry—and he decided to scrub the rest of the mission right then and there (2 Samuel 6:8-11).

What in the world went wrong? Would you believe they were carrying the ark wrong? Believe it. A few centuries earlier God had actually given Moses detailed instructions for how the ark was to be moved from place to place. Unfortunately, however, it seems those instructions had been lost (i.e., forgotten) while the ark had been sitting in storage all those years.

After God's wakeup call, David went back to Jerusalem, pulled out the Bible (the Law of Moses), started doing some homework, and discovered God's original instructions for how to move the ark. He discovered that God had specifically said it was to be carried by the Levites, and they were to carry it on their shoulders with gold-plated poles which were slipped through rings at the base of each corner of the ark (Exodus 25:12-15; Numbers 4:5-6, 15).

Three months later, David *restored* that practice and finally brought the ark back to where it belonged. Here's how the Bible describes his restoration of those lost instructions:

> Now David built houses for himself in the city of David; and he prepared a place for the ark of God and pitched a tent for it. Then David said, "No one is to carry the ark of God but the Levites; for the Lord chose them to carry the ark of God and to minister to Him forever." . . . Then David called for Zadok and Abiathar the priests, and for the Levites, . . . and said to them ". . . consecrate yourselves both you and your relatives, that you may bring up the ark of the Lord God of Israel to the place that I have prepared for it. Because you did not carry it at the first, the Lord our God made an outburst on us, *for we did not seek Him according to the ordi-*

nance." ... The sons of the Levites carried the ark of God on their shoulders with the poles thereon, *as Moses had commanded according to the word of the Lord* (1 Chronicles 15:2, 11-15).

Whatever you do, don't miss the two statements which I highlighted in that passage. In the first one, David confesses that when they tried to move the ark in round one, they didn't do it God's way. His words: "We did not seek Him according to the ordinance." In the second, he acknowledges that, for round two, they *restored* God's original plan. They did it, he said, "as Moses had commanded according to the word of the Lord."

There you have it—a couple of Biblical examples of *restoration* in action. We could look at more, but I think these two get the point across. I think they give you a good sense of what we in churches of Christ mean when we talk about *restoration*. I also think they help you understand why we're convinced that the idea of restoration is so important.

Now let's take this idea of restoration over to the New Testament and focus our conversation on the church.

THAT'S A PATTERN

To help you begin getting your mind wrapped around our goal of restoring Jesus's true church, I think the best place to start is by telling you that we believe the New Testament contains a general pattern of beliefs and practices that God expects every local church to follow.

But don't bother looking through your New Testament for the place where all the details of this pattern are neatly laid out. Don't bother because it's not neatly laid out in one particular place.

Instead, it's found in the overall teaching of the New Testament. Let me show you a few examples of what I mean.

In 1 Corinthians 14 Paul lays down some rules for who could speak to the church assembly at Corinth. He begins his instructions with these words: "As in all the congregations of the saints" (1 Corinthians 14:33b). When it came to who could speak to the assembly, the Corinthians weren't allowed to do their own thing. Paul required them to follow the same rules that "all the congregations of the saints" followed. Paul expected his speaking-in-church policy to be the same from church to church to church. That's a pattern.

Now to Acts 14. While on his first missionary journey in Asia Minor (modern Turkey), Paul and his co-worker, Barnabas, planted churches in the cities of Lystra, Iconium, and Antioch. Later, after moving on to a place called Derbe and planting a church there, the missionary duo decided to backtrack so they could strengthen and encourage the churches they had recently planted (Acts 14:20-22). On that return visit, the Bible says, "Paul and Barnabas appointed elders for them in each church" (Acts 14:23). Don't miss the words "in each church." Paul wanted "each church"—that is, each congregation—to have elders (see also Philippians 1:1; Acts 15:2; Acts 20:17). That's a pattern.

You'll find still another piece of this pattern in 1 Corinthians 16 when Paul tells the church at Corinth: "Now about the collection for God's people: Do what I told the Galatian churches to do. On the first day of every week, each one of you should set aside a sum of money in keeping with his income, . . ." (1 Corinthians 16:1-2). Notice that Paul gave the church in Corinth the exact same instructions that he gave all the churches in the region of Galatia, which happens to be several hundred miles east of Corinth.[2]

All these churches were meeting on the first day of every week, and all were told to take up a collection on that day in order to meet a need. By the way, in Acts 20 you'll see that the church in Troas also met together on the first day of the week (Acts 20:6-7).[3] The fact that all these churches met together on the first day of every week is either an unplanned coincidence or a God-planned pattern. We believe it's a God-planned pattern.

Let me show just one more piece of this pattern. In 1 Timothy 2 Paul lays down some more rules for church assemblies. One of those rules is, "I want the men in every place to pray, lifting up holy hands, without wrath and dissention" (1 Timothy 2:8). Notice that his command for male Christians[4] to pray was to be carried out "in every place." Bible scholars have pointed out that this phrase was used in somewhat of a technical sense to mean "in every place of meeting."[5] In every place where Christians met to worship God and encourage one another, Paul wanted men whose lives were characterized by holy living to lead the congregation in prayer. Paul expected this command to be carried out "in every place." That's a pattern.

Maybe you've never really thought much about it before, but now can you see that there really is a general pattern in the New Testament that God wants His people to follow? In other words, can you see that God wants some things to be the same in every congregation? If you can see that, then you're seeing the foundational belief that motivates us in our quest to restore Jesus's true church. But there's more. There's also a second important belief that helps drive us toward this goal.

The very fact that we're calling for a *restoration* of New Testament beliefs and practices means we believe many of those beliefs and practices have been lost. In other words, we believe most church groups today have lost some important parts of God's revealed pattern for His local church. Some groups are definitely closer to conforming to that general pattern than others, but, unfortunately, we feel most church groups fall short of conforming to it in some significant areas.

When I say this, though, I want you to know that I have the utmost respect for my denominational friends and neighbors. When I point out that most of them aren't conforming to certain parts of God's original pattern for His church, I can assure you there's not a single holier-than-thou thought in my head. Nor are there any delusions of perfection in my mind concerning churches of Christ. I'm just acknowledging the reality of what we've seen, and that is that God's original instructions can very easily be lost.

To sum it up and put it in a nutshell, most of us in churches of Christ truly believe the New Testament contains a general pattern for every local church to follow, and we're totally sold-out in our commitment to do just that. We want to conform to that pattern as fully as we possibly can. We also hope that others who want to follow Jesus will see the importance of conforming to that pattern as well, and will want to unite in a properly restored New Testament church.

NOT JUST ANOTHER DENOMINATION EITHER

Earlier I told you that we don't consider ourselves to be just another evangelical church. Now it's important to tell you that we don't consider ourselves to be just another denomination either. Do you remember earlier in the chapter when I told you that we don't want to be a denomination, and I said I'd tell you more about that later? It's later now, so let me tell you a little bit more about that.

Simply put, we don't want to be just another denomination because being a denomination doesn't conform to the New Testament model of Jesus's church. From the first chapter of the New Testament (Matthew 1) to the last (Revelation 22), you won't find the first reference to different denominations. The true church of Jesus Christ was *pre*-denominational. In other words, Jesus's church existed long before denominations began to emerge in the wake of the Protestant Reformation.

What you'll find in the New Testament is that followers of Christ simply considered themselves to be members of the church which He built and which belongs to Him (Matthew 16:18). And what you'll find in the New Testament is that Jesus's church was just a loose fellowship of independent, local congregations which were expected to conform to the same general pattern of beliefs and practices.

Following that clear New Testament model, that's what churches of Christ are—we're just a loose fellowship of independent, local congregations committed to following the same pattern of beliefs and practices that congregations in the New Testament followed.

In her book *The Unauthorized Guide to Choosing a Church*, Carmen Renee Berry rightly says that churches of Christ "have no central headquarters with no overriding organizational structure—at all."[6] She goes on to say, "I respect the way they have translated their beliefs into action. They believe the original church was organized around local congregations. Other groups agree with this idea but go right ahead and organize denominations anyway."[7] She then says churches of Christ are "more consistent in living out their beliefs, in my opinion, than any other in this regard."[8]

In the back of her book, you'll find a list of thirty-five church groups with their official website. "Churches of Christ" is the only one of those thirty-five groups with "no web site."[9] And in her chapter on churches of Christ, she mentions how, in spite of no formal organization, they've done things like create several colleges and establish homes for abandoned children and the elderly. She then says, "Not bad for a group that can't be called up on the phone."[10] Why does she say churches of Christ "can't be called up on the phone"? Because there is no denomination called "The Church of Christ." Again, we're just a loose fellowship of independent congregations.

When most of us refer to our home congregation as "a church of Christ" we're not saying that we belong to a denomination called "The Church of Christ." While most people who hear me say, "I'm a member of a church of Christ," no doubt take it as a reference to a denomination, I'm actually trying to use "church of Christ" the same way Paul did when he told the church in Rome that "all the churches of Christ send greetings" (Romans

16:16). When he said that, he wasn't referring to congregations which were part of a denomination called "The Church of Christ"; he was simply referring to every congregation that belongs to Christ and follows the same general pattern of beliefs and practices. And that's what I'm trying to say my home congregation is.

NON-DENOMINATIONAL? YES AND NO

"Obviously, then, this means churches of Christ are non-denominational churches, right?" The answer to that question is actually both "Yes" and "No." Since every congregation in our fellowship is 100% independent, and since there's absolutely no formal organizational structure beyond any local congregation, every church of Christ definitely embraces being non-denominational as part of its identity.

However—and this is an important *however*—churches of Christ are *not* non-denominational in the same sense that others claim to be non-denominational. Most churches that identify themselves as non-denominational actually see nothing wrong with the concept of dividing God's church into different denominations. While they choose to be non-denominational themselves, they genuinely believe God is equally pleased with or without denominational structures in His church.

We in churches of Christ, however, are not just non-denominational, but we're also *anti*-denominational. Of course this doesn't mean we're opposed to the people in denominational churches. I love my denominational friends and neighbors. Most of them are wonderful, God-fearing, Bible-believing people trying their best to serve God with a sincere heart. When I say we're *anti*-denominational, I just mean we're opposed to the whole concept of dividing believers into different denominations. We actually wish no denominations existed. We genuinely believe God is *not* pleased with dividing His church into different denominations.

Why are we so opposed to the concept of denominations? For one thing, as I pointed out earlier, different denominations are conspicuously absent in the New Testament. I think that's a pretty strong piece of evidence that God doesn't want His people divided into different denominations.

For another thing—and I'm convinced this explains why there are no denominations in the New Testament—there's the New Testament's appeal for unity and its condemnation of division in God's church. For instance, the apostle Paul rebukes the church in Corinth for beginning to divide and identify themselves by different names. Here's what he wrote:

> I appeal to you, brothers, in the name of our Lord Jesus Christ, that all of you agree with one another so that there may be no divisions among you and that you may be perfectly united in mind and thought. My brothers, some from Chloe's household have informed me that there are quarrels among you. What I mean is this: One of you says, "I follow Paul"; another, "I follow Apollos"; another, "I follow Cephas"; still another, "I follow Christ." Is Christ divided? Was Paul crucified for you? Were you baptized into the name of Paul? (1 Corinthians 1:10-13).

Then, of course, there are the words of Jesus Himself which are surely relevant when considering whether it's appropriate to divide God's people into different denominations. Just a few hours before His arrest and execution, He prayed, "My prayer is not for them alone [the apostles]. I pray also for those who will believe in me through their message, that all of them may be one, Father, just as you are in me and I am in you. May they also be in us so that the world may believe that you have sent me" (John 17:20-21). Can anyone seriously argue that dividing Jesus's people into different denominations honors His expressed desire for oneness among them?

Among the membership of most churches of Christ you'll discover that many are former members of various denominational church groups. Both of my parents and my wife's parents fall into that category. Many made the difficult decision to leave their respective denominations when they came to see the importance of conforming to God's revealed pattern for His church. When, among other things, they learned that dividing people into different denominations wasn't a part of God's New Testament pattern, they decided to live out that belief. They were determined to make whatever changes were necessary in order to more fully conform to the same simple pattern that every church in the New Testament was expected to follow. In churches of Christ they sure didn't find perfection, but they did find that same determination.

Now that you know about our goal of restoring the beliefs and practices of the church in the New Testament, I'm ready to show you how that goal has led us to embrace a few beliefs and practices that distinguish us from most of our evangelical neighbors.

CHAPTER 2

SALVATION & CHURCH MEMBERSHIP IN THE SHAPE OF THE NEW TESTAMENT

The first Pentecost in Jerusalem after Jesus walked out of His tomb began like every other Pentecost. It looked like Pentecost. It smelled like Pentecost. It sounded like Pentecost. But it sure didn't end like every other Pentecost. When this one was over, this centuries-old Jewish festival would be more closely associated with Christianity than Judaism because it was on that day, in that place, that God first began offering salvation in the name of Jesus Christ to every person on the face of the earth.

Thanks to Luke, you can read the dramatic details of that day in Acts 2, and one of those dramatic details is that God saved about three thousand people and added them to His church (Acts 2:41). Luke then closes the chapter a few verses later with this announcement: "And the Lord added to their number daily those who were being saved" (Acts 2:47).

With Luke's incredible evangelism reports firmly in mind, I'd like you to ponder a few questions. What conditions did those three thousand converts on the Day of Pentecost have to meet before God saved them and added them to His church? And in the days that followed Pentecost, when new people were being saved and added to Jesus's church every day, what conditions did those people have to meet before God saved them and added them to the church? And what exactly do we have to do before God will save us and add us to Jesus's church?

Our answer to these questions reveals the most important difference you'll find between churches of Christ and most evangelical church groups. It's not the *only* important difference, but it is, as I said, the *most* important difference.

Our answer begins with a confessed belief. Before the Lord will save us and add us to His church, we believe the Bible teaches that we must be totally convinced of a few fundamental truths, like these:

- Our sins have placed us under the wrath of the infinitely holy God, and our destiny, as sinners, is eternal separation from Him in hell.

- Despite our sins, God loves us, doesn't want to send us to hell, and He alone can change our lost condition; we're completely powerless to save ourselves.

- God can save us because He punished Jesus in our place. God put all our sins on Jesus and poured out on Him all the holy wrath that our sins deserve by nailing Him to a cross.

- After Jesus died on the cross as a substitute for us, His body was taken down and buried, but three days later He came back to life by the power of God.

It's not enough, though, just to be convinced in our mind that these things are true. We also have to be willing to verbally confess our conviction that Jesus is the crucified and resurrected Savior of the world. Frankly, though, this part of our salvation-answer doesn't distinguish us from most evangelicals. Most evangelicals are on the same page as far as this condition of salvation goes. Obviously, then, there's more to our answer than just a verbally confessed conviction about the nature and work of Christ.

If we want God to save us and add us to His church, we also believe the Bible teaches that we must stop living in sin, and surrender ourselves to a life of obedience to God. The Bible calls this *repentance*. But this part of our salvation-answer doesn't really distinguish us from most evangelicals either. A lot of evangelicals also believe repentance is necessary for salvation. This means, of course, there's still more to our answer.

In addition to a confessed belief and repentance, we also believe God has mandated baptism as a condition for receiving salvation and being added to His church. With a heart full of faith in Jesus's saving work on the cross, and a firm commitment to live life God's way, we believe God forgives our sins, gives us His Holy Spirit, and adds us to His church the moment we're baptized into the death of Christ and raised in the likeness of His resurrection. Baptism, in other words, *completes* our response of saving faith.

Our full and final salvation-answer, then, *begins* with a confessed belief, *continues* with repentance, and is *completed* in baptism.

It's where our salvation-answer is completed—in the water of Christian baptism—that the road forks between those of us in churches of Christ and most of our evangelical neighbors. As passionately as we embrace baptism as a necessary condition for salvation and church membership, most of our evangelical and

Protestant friends passionately reject the notion that it's necessary for salvation.

THE "PICK YOUR BATTLES" CHALLENGE

We've all heard the phrase "pick your battles," and I'll admit those words have been some of the best counsel I've ever given . . . and received. Those three little words just seem to have a magical way of forcing us to pause in the middle of an intensely emotional moment and ask ourselves, "Is this really an issue, or a belief, that I need to dig a foxhole and fight to the death over? Or is it something I can compromise on?"

What about this belief of ours that baptism is absolutely essential for salvation? Are we in churches of Christ stubbornly clinging to a belief that we should be willing to move away from for the sake of deeper unity with our Bible-believing friends who don't share that belief? I've actually pondered that question quite a bit, and I've concluded that it really is a foxhole-and-fight conviction.

Don't let that language throw you though. I don't mean "fight" in the sense of being ungracious, unkind, and harsh in defense of it. I hope my defense of this belief, or any belief for that matter, will always be done with a gracious spirit. I just mean, if God has joined baptism and salvation together—and I'm convinced He has—then we simply cannot allow them to be separated, even for something as desirable as closer fellowship with others who seek to honor Jesus as their Lord.

Let me show you why I believe this and I'll start by pointing you to one of the most terrifying passages in the Bible—at least

I'm convinced it's one of the most terrifying. Early in Jesus's ministry, as He was winding down the Sermon on the Mount, He dropped this bomb on the crowd:

> Not everyone who says to me, "Lord, Lord," will enter the kingdom of heaven, but the one who does the will of my Father who is in heaven. On that day many will say to me, "Lord, Lord, did we not prophesy in your name, and cast out demons in your name, and do many mighty works in your name?" And then I will declare to them, "I never knew you; depart from me, you workers of lawlessness" (Matthew 7:21-23).

With those spine-tingling words, Jesus made it impossibly clear that people can actually believe they're saved, but in reality be lost . . . people who not only genuinely believe He's their Lord, but who also are active in serving Him and promoting His cause. Now *that's* scary.

If you ask me, those words should be enough to make anyone want to revisit their salvation while they're still breathing. I'm definitely not suggesting that we should walk around every day with a big question mark dogging us about our salvation, but Jesus's words definitely suggest that we shouldn't take our salvation for granted either.

Why did Jesus say *many*—His word, not mine—who acknowledge and serve Him as Lord in this life will be lost on the day of judgment? In a word, the reason is *disobedience*. To use His words, it'll be because they failed to do "the will of my Father." Jesus then followed up this attention-getting announcement with an exhortation to take obedience to God very seriously, and He did it with one of His most memorable parables, the parable of the wise and foolish builders (Matthew 7:24-27). If your Bible is in arms reach, it wouldn't hurt to take about thirty seconds to flip to that passage and read those four verses.

With this obedience-wake-up-call ringing in our ears, I want to throw out a couple of Old Testament stories for us to think about. The first is the familiar story of Jericho in Joshua 6.

On D-Day of the Israelite invasion of the Promised Land, the first target was the walled Canaanite city of Jericho, and God's plan of attack was a bit unorthodox—the army of Israel was to march around Jericho for seven consecutive days. For the first six days, God ordered them to march around the town once a day. Included in the march was to be seven priests who would each carry a ram's horn in front of the ark of the covenant. On day seven, He ordered them to march around the town seven times, after which the priests were to blow their rams' horns and the people were to shout as loudly as possible. God promised that the walls of the city would collapse the moment His orders were carried out, and Jericho would be theirs for the taking (Joshua 6:3-5).

Here's a question for you now: What if the Israelites had done everything precisely as God commanded *except* for one simple thing? What if, on the last day, they had marched around Jericho six times instead of seven? Do you think God still would have brought down the walls? I've asked that question to quite a few people throughout my life and ministry, and if you're like 99.9% of them, then you're thinking, "Of course not." And if that's what you're thinking, then your thinking is right on target. Nothing in the Bible leads us to believe that *close* obedience would have been close enough during that Jericho mission. The clear implication of the text is that Israel had to meet *every* condition that God attached to His promise to bring down those walls.

Our second story is probably a notch or two lower on most people's scale of familiarity, but it's still one of the well-known stories in the Old Testament. It's found in 2 Kings 5, and the leading man is an Aramean general who was eaten up with the horribly disfiguring disease of leprosy. His name is Naaman and, in search of a miracle, he packed his bags and headed south into Israel looking for the prophet Elisha.

Cutting right to the chase, Elisha told Naaman to "go and wash in the Jordan seven times, and your flesh will be restored to you and you will be clean" (2 Kings 5:10). The story then closes like this: "So he went down and dipped himself seven times in the Jordan according to the word of the man of God; and his flesh was restored like the flesh of a little child and he was clean" (2 Kings 5:14).

Here's your next question: Do you think Naaman would have been healed if he had stopped after the sixth dip in the Jordan? I don't think I'm going out on a limb to assume you're thinking, once again, "Of course not." And if that's what you're thinking, then, once again, I'm convinced you nailed it. Just as close obedience would not have cut it on the Jericho mission, it would not have cut it in Naaman's case either. The clear implication of the text is that Naaman had to meet *every* condition that God attached to His promise to heal him.

Stories like these are very instructive, and one of the most important lessons they teach is that it's critical to meet *every* condition that God attaches to a promise. By the way, insisting that all of God's conditions must be met is *not* a sign of legalism . . . it's a sign of faith. Stay tuned for a few more words about faith a little later, but for now let me give you this verse to chew on: "By faith the walls of Jericho fell down after they had been encircled for seven days" (Hebrews 11:30).

Like God's promise to give the Israelites victory at Jericho and His promise to heal Naaman of leprosy, His promise to save us from our sins through the blood of Christ comes with conditions attached. And if He made baptism one of those conditions, then no one has the authority to dismiss it . . . for *any* reason.

That, of course, is precisely where we in churches of Christ stand. Since we believe baptism is one of the conditions that God has attached to His promise of salvation, we can't dismiss it anymore than Israel or Naaman could have dismissed any of the conditions that God attached to His promises to them.

CHURCH "YES," SALVATION "NO"?

In the rest of this chapter I'm going to do my best to show you that our belief fits the teaching of the New Testament, and I want to start by going back to the last statement I made in the first section of this chapter. Here it is again: "As passionately as we embrace baptism as a necessary condition for salvation and church membership, most of our evangelical and Protestant neighbors passionately reject it as a necessary condition for salvation."

Did you notice I said we believe baptism is a necessary condition for salvation *and* church membership . . . and then I said most evangelical and Protestant church groups reject baptism as necessary for salvation . . . *but I didn't say they reject it as necessary for church membership?* That omission was no oversight on my part. I purposely left that last part out because many church groups that reject baptism as necessary for salvation actually teach that it *is* necessary to be a member of the Lord's church . . . *and* to participate in the Lord's Supper.

With the utmost respect for my Bible-believing friends who hold this view, I'm convinced that it's biblically impossible to insist that baptism *is not* necessary for salvation, and at the same time insist that it *is* necessary for membership in God's saved community—the church—and for participation in the Lord's Supper.

Simply put, being saved and belonging to God's saved community are not separated in the Bible. In other words, the notion that a person can be saved and still *not* be a member of Jesus's church is completely unknown in the New Testament. Just take another look—a slow, deliberate look—at Luke's last statement in Acts 2: "And the Lord was adding to their number day by day those who were being saved" (Acts 2:47).

Notice that, according to Luke, the Lord was saving people and adding them to His saved community at the exact same moment. May I suggest that if being saved and being added to God's saved community happens simultaneously, then whatever conditions are necessary for one are necessary for the other. That means, of course, if baptism is a necessary condition for church membership, then it's also a necessary condition for salvation.

The same is true of the Lord's Supper. The notion that a person can be saved but still *not* be allowed to come to the Lord's table with the Lord's people to eat the Lord's Supper simply doesn't fit New Testament teaching. The New Testament assumes that every person who is in *covenant* with God (i.e., saved) will regularly gather with the *covenant* community (i.e., the church) to eat the *covenant* meal (i.e., the Lord's Supper). So, whatever conditions a person must meet in order to eat the covenant meal are the same conditions a person must meet in order to be in covenant with God. And that adds up to one thing—if baptism is a necessary condition for eating the Lord's Supper, then it's also a necessary condition for salvation.

A LITTLE HELP FROM HISTORY

As I continue to build a case for our belief that baptism is necessary for salvation and church membership, I want to offer up as evidence the fact that this was the unanimous belief of Christianity for its first 1,500 years—give or take a few years.

Hopefully you remember my blurb in the first chapter about the Protestant Reformation and men like Martin Luther who led that reform movement. Another man at the point of the Reformation spear was Huldreich Zwingli, and in the early 1500s he came to the bold conclusion that every Bible teacher before him had been wrong about baptism. Specifically, he concluded they had been wrong in their belief that baptism is necessary for salvation.

Just listen to Zwingli's own acknowledgement that he was going against 1,500 years of agreement: "In this matter of baptism, I can only conclude that all the doctors have been in error from the time of the apostles. . . . For all the doctors have ascribed to water a power which it does not have and the holy apostles did not teach."[1] He went on to say, "The Fathers were in error . . . because they thought that the water itself effects cleansing and salvation."[2]

These statements seem to make it crystal clear that there was a consensus about the meaning and purpose of baptism from the time of the apostles until Zwingli, and that consensus was that baptism is the time and place that God forgives and saves.[3]

I've often heard supporters of "infant sprinkling" and supporters of "believer's immersion" square off over which of these two views has "historical precedent." That is, did the earliest Christians sprinkle infants, or did they immerse only those who first expressed faith in Christ? A completely honest look at church history reveals that "believer's immersion" wins that argument.

But there's another view that has even more historical precedent than "believer's immersion," and that view is "believer's immersion *for the forgiveness of sins*." Historians who specialize in early church history will not only confirm that the earliest Christians immersed believers only, but they'll also confirm that they immersed them *for the forgiveness of sins*.

What's my point? The point is that a good history check provides an important way to test our interpretation of the New Testament. If we come to a conclusion about what the New Testament teaches concerning a particular subject, but then discover that our conclusion goes against long-held Christian beliefs, then we really should take a closer look at our interpretation.

Of course I'm not suggesting that church history should determine our understanding of the Bible. Hear me well—church history must *never* be our ultimate authority when it comes to determining our beliefs and practices. That role is reserved only for the Bible. My point is, as one writer put it, "long-held traditions in the church should not be jettisoned casually or without careful reflection, for we are all liable to the chronological snobbery of the modern age and apt to dismiss the contribution of thoughtful Christians who have preceded us."[4]

With that said, the fact that the earliest Christians believed that baptism was for the forgiveness of sins, and the fact that every Bible teacher believed the same thing until Zwingli came onto the scene in the early sixteenth century, should make us want to take a good hard look at the popular, contemporary belief that baptism is *not* for the forgiveness of sins.

Let me take you back to Zwingli for a moment because there are still a couple of blanks in this story that need to be filled in. The first blank is what Zwingli came to believe about baptism after he rejected the 1,500 year consensus that it was the time and place that God forgives and saves. To make a long story really, really short, he taught that baptism has two basic purposes.

First, he taught that baptism is essentially a public announcement which is mostly for the benefit of the church. According to Zwingli, it's a person's announcement to his fellow Christians that he or she is joining them in their commitment to serve Jesus. This is where the popular belief that baptism is a "public testimony" or "public witness" comes from.

Second, he taught that baptism is simply a sign that one belongs to God's new covenant community, the church. In other words, Zwingli taught that baptism was the new version of Old Testament circumcision. He argued that just as circumcision was the outward sign that a person belonged to God's old covenant community, baptism is now the outward sign that a person belongs to His new covenant community. By the way, Zwingli came to this particular conclusion while developing his rationale for infant baptism.[5]

The second blank that needs to be filled-in is what happened in the aftermath of Zwingli's proposed new meaning of baptism. Zwingli didn't live long after he formulated his new doctrine of baptism, but his view was adopted by another influential Reformer named John Calvin and it became part of a doctrinal system called Reformed theology. That system of doctrine was then adopted by most denominations that emerged from the Reformation. And that's why most who trace their spiritual roots to the Reformation still reject the idea that baptism is for the forgiveness of sins. It really all goes back to Zwingli.

BAPTISM AND SALVATION: A CLEAR CONNECTION

Now the question I want you to think about is this: Why did every Bible teacher for the first 1,500 years of Christian history believe that baptism is necessary for salvation? The answer is pretty simple. They believed it because the most natural, most straightforward meaning of so many New Testament passages link baptism and salvation together. Incidentally, that not only explains why *they* believed baptism is necessary for salvation, but it also explains why *we* in churches of Christ believe it too.

With that said, though, I sure don't expect you to just take my word that the New Testament repeatedly links baptism with salvation. It's important for you to see this connection for yourself, so let's take a look at a few New Testament passages. As we do this, let me encourage you to let the words of these passages just say what they say. In other words, just accept the most natural, most straightforward meaning of the words. If you'll do that, I think you'll have to admit that the connection between baptism and salvation is glaring.

ACTS 2:38

"Repent and be baptized, every one of you, in the name of Jesus for the forgiveness of your sins. And you will receive the gift of the Holy Spirit" (Acts 2:38).

First, some background. We're back to where we started this chapter—on the Day of Pentecost and the very beginning of the church. We're back to the very moment when forgiveness of sins through Jesus was first offered and first received. And here we find the apostle Peter, filled with the Holy Spirit, preaching the very first gospel sermon.

When that Pentecost crowd believed everything Peter told them about Jesus, their hearts melted, they asked him and the other apostles what they needed to do, and they heard these words come out of Peter's mouth: "Repent and be baptized, every one of you, in the name of Jesus for the forgiveness of your sins. And you will receive the gift of the Holy Spirit" (Acts 2:38).

From time to time when I'm studying the Bible with someone, and we're discussing salvation, this is one of the verses we'll read together. After we read it, I always ask, "What does Peter tell the crowd to do in order to have their sins forgiven?" Without exception, the reply has always been, "Repent and be baptized."

Why do you think people always reply that way? Why do you think they always say, "Repent and be baptized"? It's because they just let Peter's words say what they say. That is, they just accept the most straightforward, most natural meaning of his words, and the most straightforward, most natural meaning connects baptism with the forgiveness of sins.

ACTS 22:16

"And now why do you delay? Arise, and be baptized, and wash away your sins, calling on His name" (Acts 22:16).

Here's the background of this verse. A blind, guilt-ridden Saul (soon to be the apostle Paul) asked the risen Jesus, "What shall I do, Lord?" (Acts 22:10). Jesus told him to go into the city of Damascus and someone would tell him what to do. He goes. He waits. He fasts. He prays.

Three days later, a man named Ananias pays him a visit. During that visit, Ananias miraculously heals Paul's blindness, informs the ex-persecutor that he's been selected to be an apostle of God, and then says to him, "Why do you delay? Arise, and be baptized, and wash away your sins, calling on His name" (Acts 22:16).

Does Ananias say, "Arise and be baptized to symbolize that God has already washed your sins away"? He doesn't, does he? Does he say, "Arise and be baptized as a public testimony to your fellow Christians that you are now one of them"? He doesn't say that either, does he? He says, "Arise, and be baptized, and wash away your sins." Doesn't the most straightforward meaning of those words link baptism with the washing away of sins?

MATTHEW 28:19-20

> "Go therefore and make disciples of all the nations, baptizing them in the name of the Father and the Son and the Holy Spirit, teaching them to observe all that I commanded you; and lo, I am with you always, even to the end of the age" (Matthew 28:19-20).

This is the first mention of Christian baptism in the New Testament, and most people call these verses "the Great Commission." Here Jesus gives His apostles their marching orders, and those orders are to "go . . . and make disciples of all the nations."

Jesus then tells them how to actually make a disciple, and He summarizes the process in two steps: (1) baptizing them in the name of the Father, Son, and Holy Spirit, and (2) teaching them to observe everything that Jesus commanded.

If you accept the most natural, most straightforward meaning of these disciple-making orders, can you really say that a person can become a disciple—that is, a Christian—without being baptized? You can't really say that, can you? Doesn't the most natural, most straightforward meaning of Jesus's words link baptism with becoming a disciple?

MARK 16:15-16

"And He said to them, 'Go into all the world and preach the gospel to all creation. He who has believed and has been baptized shall be saved; but he who has disbelieved shall be condemned" (Mark 16:15-16).

These two verses are part of a larger section—Mark 16:9-20— that not everyone believes was an original part of Mark's gospel. That's why most translations put brackets around this section and add a footnote which says something like, "Some of the earliest manuscripts do not include 16:9-20." Personally, however, I don't think the case for rejecting these verses is an open-and-shut case.[6] In fact, at this point in my studies, I believe Mark really wrote these seventeen verses. For arguments sake, then, I'm assuming Mark was really quoting Jesus when he wrote: "He who has believed and has been baptized shall be saved."

This is another one of those passages where people always say the same thing when I ask, "What does Jesus say that a person must do in order to be saved?" The answer I always get is, "Believe and be baptized." Why do people always say that? Again, it's because they just let Jesus's words say what they say. In other words, they just accept the most straightforward, most natural meaning of His words, and the most straightforward meaning of His words connects baptism and salvation.

ROMANS 6:3-4

"Or do you not know that all of us who have been baptized into Christ Jesus have been baptized into His death? Therefore we have been buried with Him through baptism into death, in order that as Christ was raised from the dead through the glory of the Father, so we too might walk in newness of life" (Romans 6:3-4).

In the first part of Romans 6 Paul is explaining to the Christians at Rome why they can't purposely live sinful lifestyles. The reason is because each of them had died to their old life which was controlled by sinful desires, and each had been given a new spiritual life.

And that brings us to verses 3 and 4. In these verses, Paul reminds them of the actual moment they died to sin and received new life. That moment, according to him, was when they were "baptized into Christ Jesus." Again, here's what he said: "Or do you not know that *all of us who have been baptized into Christ Jesus have been baptized into His death*? Therefore *we have been buried with Him through baptism into death, in order that . . . we too might walk in newness of life.*"

Notice that Paul doesn't say they died to their old life and rose to a new life when they "asked Jesus into their heart" (as some Bible-believers teach). And notice that he doesn't say they spiritually died and rose again when they "said a sinner's prayer" (as others teach). And please notice that he doesn't say their baptism was just a symbol of their spiritual death and resurrection which really took place at some earlier time (as many teach).

If we just accept Paul's words "as is," he points directly to baptism as the actual time and place when two incredible things happen. It's the time and place that a person actually dies to their old sinful life, and actually rises to a new redeemed life. And if baptism is the actual moment that a person dies with Christ and is raised to walk in a new life, aren't baptism and salvation connected?

GALATIANS 3:26-27

"For you are all sons of God through faith in Christ Jesus. For all of you who were baptized into Christ have clothed yourselves with Christ" (Galatians 3:26-27).

"Baptized into Christ." If that expression sounds familiar, it's because you just saw it. In Romans 6:3 Paul tells every Christian in Rome that they were "baptized into Christ," and here he tells every Christian in every congregation throughout the province of Galatia that they were "baptized into Christ" as well.

If you accept the most natural, most straightforward meaning of that expression—"baptized into Christ"—what does it sound like Paul is saying? Does it sound like nothing actually happens at the moment of baptism? Not exactly, does it? Does it sound like baptism is just symbolic of some earlier time—maybe a week earlier, or a month earlier, or even a year earlier—when God united us with Christ? It doesn't sound like that either, does it?

Doesn't the most straightforward meaning of those words suggest that, in our faith, God actually places us in Christ at the moment of our baptism? We are all "baptized into Christ," Paul plainly says. But there's more. He adds, "For all of you who were baptized into Christ *have clothed yourselves with Christ*."

That's an incredibly vivid image. Christ is compared with clothing that we put on and begin to wear. Surely this image is meant to convey the idea of being in union with Christ. When we put on Christ in baptism, we become a part of Christ. When we put on Christ in baptism, we become one with Him. When we put on Christ in baptism, we belong to Him. And if baptism is the actual moment that we're clothed with Christ, aren't baptism and salvation connected?

COLOSSIANS 2:11-13

"And in Him you were also circumcised with a circumcision made without hands, in the removal of the body of the flesh by the circumcision of Christ; having been buried with Him in baptism, in which you were also raised up with Him through faith in the working of God, who raised Him from the dead. And when you were dead in your transgressions and the uncircumcision of your flesh, He made you alive together with Him, having forgiven us all our transgressions" (Colossians 2:11-13).

Here's another vivid image. It's the image of God performing spiritual surgery. Just as a doctor removes physical flesh in the operation of circumcision, God removes spiritual flesh (i.e., sin) in a spiritual operation. The question for us, of course, is when does God perform this operation on a person?

If we accept the most straightforward meaning of these verses, Paul says God does it "*in* baptism"—not *before* baptism or *after* baptism. And not only that, he says "*in* baptism"—again, not *before* or *after* baptism—we are "raised up with Him [Christ] through faith in the working of God." Let's read it again: "And ***in Him you*** *were also circumcised* . . . in the removal of the body of the flesh by the circumcision of Christ; *having been buried with Him in baptism, in which you were also raised up with Him through faith in the working of God,* who raised Him from the dead."

If we take these words "as is," then baptism is the actual moment when God meets us in our faith and cuts away our sins. And if we take these words "as is," then baptism is the actual moment when God meets us in our faith and raises us up to a new, forgiven life. And if baptism is the actual moment that God removes our sinful flesh, raises us from spiritual death, and makes us alive together with Christ, aren't baptism and salvation connected?

1 PETER 3:21

"And corresponding to that, baptism now saves you— not the removal of dirt from the flesh, but an appeal to God for a good conscience—through the resurrection of Jesus Christ" (1 Peter 3:21).

This is the last passage we'll look at, and in it Peter compares baptism with the flood, through which eight people—Noah and his family—were safely brought through water. It's an extraordinary statement.

Now look at these four words again: "baptism now saves you." If we accept the simplest, most straightforward, most natural meaning of those words, I don't know how it's possible to deny a connection between baptism and salvation. While, according to Peter, the power behind baptism is the power of Jesus's resurrection, if we accept the most natural meaning of his words, don't we have to concede that baptism has a real role in God's plan to save people? There's definitely nothing magical about baptism, but there's definitely water in His plan.

WHAT ABOUT FAITH?

"But doesn't the Bible teach that we're saved by faith alone? If it does, then nothing else is necessary—including baptism." This is probably the number one objection leveled against our belief that baptism is a necessary condition for receiving salvation.

Let me begin by saying that the Bible absolutely, positively teaches that we're saved by faith. Paul, for instance, says, "Therefore, since we have been justified through faith, we have peace with God through our Lord Jesus Christ" (Romans 5:1). Then there's the most well-known verse in the New Testament, if not the whole Bible, which says, "For God so loved the world, that he gave his only Son, that whoever believes in him should not perish but have eternal life" (John 3:16).[7] And we could go on and on.

However—and this is another huge *however*—a statement like "baptism can't be necessary if we're saved by faith alone" signals a major misunderstanding of faith. Many who make this kind of statement have been taught that faith is essentially nothing more than believing in your mind that something is true. Consequently, they've been taught that having faith in Christ simply means being convinced in your mind that He's the crucified, resurrected Savior.[8]

In the Bible, however, faith is more than just an intellectual conviction that something is true. In the Bible, the word "faith" is often used as a single-word summary to describe a response to God that combines conviction *and* action. In the Bible, genuine faith only happens when a person: (1) believes what God tells them (conviction) *and* (2) obeys the commands He gives them (action). That's why James says, "faith by itself, if it does not have works, is dead" (James 2:17). He simply means that real faith doesn't exist without obedience. And Paul was saying the same thing when he coined the expression "obedience of faith" (Romans 1:5; 16:26).

This faith-obedience connection really stands out in the book of Hebrews when we're reminded that many of the Israelites who came out of Egypt weren't allowed to enter the Promised Land. The writer of Hebrews says, "To whom did he swear that they would not enter his rest, but to those who were disobedient" (Hebrews 3:18). Then he says, "So we see that they were unable to enter because of unbelief" (Hebrews 3:19). Notice that verse 18 says they weren't allowed to enter because they were "disobedient," but verse 19 says it was "because of unbelief." Which was it, disobedience or unbelief? Take your pick because they mean the same. Where there is genuine faith, there is obedience. Where there is no obedience, there is no genuine faith.

Now watch it all come together in the verse I gave you to chew on earlier: "By faith the walls of Jericho fell after the people had marched around them for seven days" (Hebrews 11:30). Did the walls of Jericho fall by faith? Was marching around those walls for seven days, precisely as God commanded, absolutely necessary for them to collapse? I'm assuming you're thinking "yes" to both those questions.

But how could it be both? The answer is because genuine faith includes obedience. For the Israelites, faith that would bring down the walls of Jericho included obeying every command that God issued in the battle plan. For the Israelites, putting their faith in God happened when they carried out His command to march around the city for seven days. That's why the writer of Hebrews can say that the walls fell "by faith," and also say that they fell after the people carried out God's orders to march for a week.

Our salvation works the same way. In some places the Bible can simply say we're saved "through faith" (Romans 5:1), and then in other places it can say, "repent and be baptized . . . for the forgiveness of your sins" (Acts 2:38). But how can it be both? The answer is because genuine faith includes obedience. Faith that saves us includes obeying every command that God has issued in His plan to save us. Putting our faith in Christ happens when we carry out His command to "repent and be baptized."

Paul does a great job showing how saving faith and baptism go together when he says, "For you are all sons of God through faith in Christ Jesus. For all of you who were baptized into Christ have clothed yourselves with Christ" (Galatians 3:26-27). According to Paul, do we become children of God "through faith"? Of course we do. And, according to him, do we put on Christ, like putting on new clothes, when we're "baptized into Christ"? Of course we do. What's the difference? There really is no difference. Paul is saying the same thing in two different ways, and he can do that because, for him, baptism is not separate from faith, but rather a part of it. For Paul, putting one's faith in Christ happens when one obeys God's command to be baptized into Christ.

Paul's understanding that baptism is a part of one's faith response to the gospel can also be seen in the book of Acts when he asked a group of men, "Did you receive the Holy Spirit when you believed?" (Acts 19:2). When they said "no," his response to them was, "Into what then were you baptized?" (Acts 19:3). He clearly expected them to receive the Holy Spirit when they "believed" *and* when they were baptized. He expected that because, for him, baptism isn't something separate from belief, but rather a part of it. For Paul, believing in Jesus happens when one is baptized into Christ.

Let me sum up by repeating what I said a moment ago. In the Bible, the word "faith" is often used as a single-word summary to describe a response to God that combines conviction *and* action. Scripture clearly shows that genuine faith only happens when we: (1) believe what God tells us (conviction) *and* (2) obey the commands He gives us (action). When we apply this to our salvation, it means that faith includes obeying every condition that God has attached to His promise to save us through the work of Jesus.

Do we in churches of Christ believe we're saved through faith alone in Jesus Christ? Absolutely! Do we also believe repentance and baptism are essential for salvation? Absolutely! While that may sound contradictory to some people, for those who understand what biblical faith really is, and know what it really looks like, there's no contradiction at all.

IMMERSION ONLY

Our conviction that baptism is necessary for salvation is not our only foxhole-and-fight conviction about baptism. We're equally tenacious defenders of immersion only. In other words, we believe only immersion counts as New Testament baptism.

Our number one reason for believing this is the simple fact that the Greek words for baptism in the New Testament mean immersion. If you look in any reputable Greek lexicon (a Greek dictionary that defines New Testament words) you'll see that the verb *baptizo* (from which we get our word *baptize*) is defined with terms like *immerse, dip, plunge, sink, submerge,* and *go under.*

Actually, though, you don't really have to spend much time in the reference section of a theological library to discover that "baptize" in the New Testament means "immerse." All you really have to do is just take a close look at the New Testament.

As you read through the New Testament you'll come across statements about baptism that only make sense if it's an immersion. Mark, for instance, says Jesus "was baptized by John [the Baptist] in the Jordan" (Mark 1:9). He doesn't say Jesus was baptized *beside* the Jordan, or *at* the Jordan, or *near* the Jordan, or *with water from* the Jordan. He was baptized "*in* the Jordan." No one is sprinkled *in* a body of water. Immersion is the only mode of baptism that happens *in* a body of water.

Mark then continues his report on Jesus's baptism by saying, "And when he came up out of the water, immediately he saw the heavens being torn open and the Spirit descending on him like a dove" (Mark 1:9-10). Did you catch the words "when he came up out of the water"? Nobody "comes up out of the water" when they're sprinkled. Only immersed people "come up out of the water."

Then there's this statement in John's Gospel about the baptizing ministry of John the Baptist: "John was also baptizing at Aenon near Salim, because water was plentiful there" (John 3:23). If baptizing can be done just by sprinkling or pouring a little water on someone's head, why did John the Baptist need to find a place where "water was plentiful"? The only mode of baptism that requires plenty of water is immersion.

Finally, there's Luke's report of the Ethiopian eunuch's conversion. After Philip told the eunuch "the good news about Jesus" (Acts 8:35), the next verse says the eunuch spotted some water and asked if he could be baptized (Acts 8:36). Here's what happened next: "And he commanded the chariot to stop, and they *both went down into the water*, Philip and the eunuch, and he baptized him. And when *they came up out of the water*, the Spirit of the Lord carried Philip away . . ." (Acts 8:38-39). Again, people who are sprinkled don't "go down into the water" and "come up out of the water." Those things only happen when a person is immersed.

Some people wonder if we go too far when we insist that it's important *how* we're baptized. In other words, do we go too far by insisting that only immersion is true baptism?

Obviously, I don't think we go too far, and here's why. If you start reading through the Bible, it won't take long to see that God cares about the details of His instructions. Whether it's Nadab and Abihu and their unauthorized-fire fiasco (Leviticus 10:1-3), Moses and his whacking-the-rock blunder (Numbers 20:2-13), or David and his transporting-the-ark-the-wrong-way debacle (2

Samuel 6:1-10), the message comes through loud and clear that God expects His people to respect the details of His instructions. And that's what we in churches of Christ are determined to do— respect the details. That means, of course, we won't shrug off His specific command to be *immersed* into Christ, and we'll keep begging others not to shrug it off either.

BELIEVER'S IMMERSION

There is one more foxhole-and-fight conviction concerning baptism that I need to tell you about, and that's our belief that God doesn't save anyone at the moment of baptism unless they first believe and repent. As I said at the outset of this chapter, salvation is *completed* in baptism, but it *begins* with belief and repentance. If sincere belief and repentance are missing-in-action when a person steps into the water, then the only thing coming away from that baptism is a couple of very wet people and a couple of moderately damp towels.

As we've already seen, Peter's Spirit-filled message to the convicted Pentecost crowd was, "Repent *and* be baptized . . . for the forgiveness of your sins" (Acts 2:38). Repenting was just as necessary for receiving God's forgiveness as being baptized. Plenty of other passages in the New Testament also clearly show that true baptism is always preceded by actions like listening to the gospel, believing Jesus is the risen Lord, repenting, and confessing faith in Christ (see Acts 8:12-13; Acts 16:14, 31, 34; 18:8; Romans 10:9-10; Colossians 2:12).

What this means, of course, is that we in churches of Christ don't recognize the practice of infant baptism as true baptism. Babies and small children simply aren't capable of understanding the gospel, believing in Jesus Christ, repenting of their sins, or confessing their faith in Jesus . . . which would seem to explain why you can't find a single baby or small child being baptized in the New Testament.

With that said, though, I have to point out that some people still actually insist that there are examples of infant baptism in the New Testament. Of course they can't actually show an infant or young child being baptized, but their "proof" that it's there is pretty ingenious. In step one, they point to passages that refer to a "household" being saved or baptized.[9] In step two, they say these households *must* have included infants. And in step three they bring it all together like this: Since these households *must* have included infants, then infants *must* have been baptized too. Voila, infant baptism!

When you take a close look at these household-conversion passages, however, you'll see that the members of these households did other things too. They feared God (Acts 10:2), they listened to the gospel message (Acts 10:44; 16:32), they believed (Acts 16:34; Acts 18:8), and they rejoiced in their salvation (Acts 16:34). Frankly, I haven't met a baby or a small child yet who can pull off any of those things. It seems obvious, then, that when the New Testament speaks of a "household" being baptized, it's referring only to those in the household who were capable of hearing the gospel, believing it, repenting, and rejoicing in their salvation.

WHAT ABOUT THOSE WHO'VE BEEN BAPTIZED DIFFERENTLY?

After this discussion on baptism you may be wondering about the spiritual status of the millions of people who haven't followed the biblical model of baptism—*believer's immersion for the forgiveness of sins*. What about those who were sprinkled rather than immersed? What about those who were only "baptized" as infants? And what about those who were immersed as believing adults, but they weren't immersed for the purpose of receiving the gift of salvation and beginning a new life?

First of all, I agree with Jack Cottrell, a professor of theology at Cincinnati Bible Seminary, who observed, "It is obvious that human traditions have seriously distorted and limited the light of Scripture concerning baptism, and many sincere people have responded in good conscience to what light they have."[10]

Second, since final judgment is God's territory, I simply can't say with absolute certainty how He'll judge every single person who sincerely responded to inaccurate teaching regarding baptism. I can say, however, that I'm very content to let Him have the final word on who is and isn't saved, and that I truly hope His grace will cover many who were unintentionally baptized improperly.

Third, I can't preach and teach what I *hope* God will do. I can only preach and teach what He has clearly revealed in His Word. With that being said, I have to say that only those who have followed the clear Bible pattern of baptism can be *absolutely, positively sure* that God has forgiven them and added them to Jesus's church.

Maybe you haven't followed that clear Bible pattern, but you're still convinced in your heart that God has forgiven and saved you. If that's the case, let me encourage you not to trust your feelings. Feelings can be incredibly deceiving. Feeling saved isn't a guarantee of being saved. Don't forget the terrifying announcement of Jesus that we looked at earlier:

> Not everyone who says to me, "Lord, Lord," will enter the kingdom of heaven, but the one who does the will of my Father who is in heaven. On that day many will say to me, "Lord, Lord, did we not prophesy in your name, and cast out demons in your name, and do many mighty works in your name?" And then I will declare to them, "I never knew you; depart from me, you workers of lawlessness" (Matthew 7:21-23).

Instead of trusting your own feelings, I want to encourage you to trust only the plain teaching of the Word of God. Be like the Psalmist who said, "I trust in your word" (Psalm 119:42). So, if you haven't followed the New Testament pattern of baptism, I hope you'll want to make absolutely sure that you're right with God by doing the exact same thing that Peter told the people on Pentecost to do—with a heart full of faith, I hope you'll "repent and be baptized [immersed] . . . in the name of Jesus for the forgiveness of your sins" (Acts 2:38).

If you think you want to do that, but you're not quite sure where to turn, or maybe you just want to talk about it a little more, why don't you contact a church of Christ in your area? I know they'd love to help you.

CHAPTER 3

MUSICAL PRAISE IN THE ASSEMBLY IN THE SHAPE OF THE NEW TESTAMENT

When most people walk into an assembly of a church of Christ for the first time, it doesn't take long before they experience a bit of religious culture-shock. Not to worry though—they don't run into anything too weird. It's just that the music is very different from what they're accustomed to. Most worship services in Christian culture today are filled with sounds that are conspicuously absent in ours. What I mean is, the familiar sounds of a piano, an organ, drums, guitars, keyboards, harps, bells, horns, or any other instrument, are nowhere to be heard when we come together for worship.

The musical sound that fills our services, and bombards our first-time guests, is a sound that most American churchgoers have seldom, if ever, heard in church. It's the sound of voices—*just* voices—singing praises to God. Our musical praise is 100% vocal . . . it's all *a cappella*.

Of course I realize that most people who encounter non-instrumental worship find it to be a pretty strange practice. Now that I think about it, I probably should backtrack on what I said earlier about our guests not running into anything "too weird." *A cappella*-only praise may not be weird to us, but to a lot of folks, "weird" happens to be the adjective of choice to describe it. And who can blame them since seeing it in American church life is about as rare as seeing a triple-play in baseball.

But guess what? While *a cappella*-only praise may be virtually unheard of in today's church culture, would you believe it has been the practice of most churches since Christianity began? Would you believe that the vast majority of Christians for two thousand years have been just as rock solid in their commitment to *a cappella*-only worship as we are?

For those who might find that claim a little hard to swallow, let me walk you through the proof, and we'll start with the word *a cappella*. Most people know that *a cappella* means singing without instrumental accompaniment, but most people don't know that it's an Italian word that literally means "in chapel style," or "as in the chapel." Every time someone says "sing *a cappella*," they're literally saying, whether they know it or not, "sing like in the chapel." The irony, of course, is that most churches in America today don't sing "like in the chapel."

Why do you think we use a word that means "as in the chapel" to describe singing without instruments? I'm sure you can put two and two together all by yourself, but humor me while I connect those dots. We say *a cappella*—"as in the chapel"—to describe vocal-only singing because the music historically heard in Christian houses of worship, or chapels, was vocal-only. Now let me walk you through a CliffsNotes-version of church history so you can see this for yourself.

THE CHURCH FATHERS

Let's start with the Church Fathers. First, though, who are they? Boiled down to a couple of sentences, they were the influential theologians, teachers, and writers from the first few centuries of church history. Sometimes they're just called "the Fathers," and you'll find their names scattered along a church-history-timeline from roughly the days immediately after the apostles to around the year 600. And what were their thoughts about instruments in worship?

Music historian James McKinnon probably summed it up in one sentence as well as anyone. In addition to authoring five books on early Christian and Latin medieval music history, this former music professor at the University of North Carolina published more than a hundred articles in music journals and reference books during his distinguished career. In one of his books on early Christian music, he wrote, "The antagonism which the Fathers of the early Church displayed toward instruments has two outstanding characteristics: vehemence and uniformity."[1]

Notice the three words that professor McKinnon used to sum up the attitude of the Church Fathers toward instruments in worship—*antagonism, vehemence,* and *uniformity.* Now let them sink in. *Antagonism*—instruments in worship were *opposed* by the Church Fathers. *Vehemence*—instruments in worship were *intensely* opposed by the Church Fathers. *Uniformity*—instruments in worship were intensely opposed by *all* the Church Fathers.[2] Obviously, instruments didn't make their way into Christian worship under their watch.

When, then, did it happen? Was it right after the Church Fathers went the way of all things? Not quite. Opposition to instruments in worship definitely wasn't buried with the last Church Father. That opposition continued to be the status quo for several more centuries.

THE MIDDLE AGES

Some historians say instruments weren't used in Christian worship for about the first thousand years of church history. Take Robert Godfrey for instance—he's a church history professor as well as the president of Westminster Seminary in California. Like most Bible believers today, Godfrey has no problem with using instruments in worship. As a historian, though, he admits that "in the worship of the church it appears that for almost the first thousand years of its history no instruments were used in Christian worship."[3]

Professor Godfrey is in the ballpark, but he's actually off by about three hundred years. Historians who've looked at this subject under a microscope say that instruments didn't really start showing up in worship until the early fourteenth century, or around the year 1300. Of course this doesn't mean that no instrument ever showed up in any church until the 1300s. If you dig around hard enough and long enough, you'll find a few isolated instances of an organ being used as early as the 800s.[4] The norm at that time, however, was still vocal-only praise, and vocal-only praise remained the norm until the early 1300s.

The famous nineteenth century church historian Joseph Bingham pointed out:

Music in churches is as ancient as the apostles, but instrumental music not so: for it is now generally agreed among learned men that the use of organs came into the church since the time of Thomas Aquinas, Anno [the year] 1250.[5]

Similarly, here's what you'll find in McClintock and Strong's *Cyclopedia of Biblical, Theological and Ecclesiastical Literature*:

Students of ecclesiastical archaeology are generally agreed that instrumental music was not used in churches till a much later date; for Thomas Aquinas, A.D. 1250, has these remarkable words: 'Our Church does not use musical instruments, as harps and psalteries, to praise God . . .' From this passage we are surely warranted in concluding that there was no ecclesiastical use of organs in the time of Aquinas.[6]

I'm sure you noticed that both Bingham and McClintock/ Strong pointed to Thomas Aquinas as a reference point for determining when instruments began making a regular appearance in Christian worship. In case the name Thomas Aquinas doesn't ring a bell, he was the most influential Roman Catholic theologian of the Middle Ages. In fact, many Catholics still consider him to be their greatest theologian and philosopher ever.

As McClintock and Strong pointed out, it's a statement that Aquinas made in 1250 which allows historians to say with confidence that instruments still weren't being used in worship at that time. Here's a bit more of what Aquinas actually said:

The Church does not use musical instruments such as the harp or lyre when praising God, in case she should seem

> to fall back into Judaism . . . For musical instruments usually move the soul more to pleasure than create inner moral goodness . . .[7]

Think about that for a minute. By the time of Thomas Aquinas, Christians had been worshiping for over 1,200 years, and one of the few practices that remained remarkably constant over that entire period of time was vocal-only praise . . . but things were about to change.

Not only did instruments start showing up in worship with increasing regularity in the 1300s, but historians report that, by the early 1500s, organs had become a fixture in almost every important church building in Europe. Keep in mind, of course, that this all happened in the Roman Catholic Church because Catholicism was the only game in town throughout most of Western Europe at that time.

Organs hadn't been a fixture in Catholic worship for long, however, when those pesky Reformers started showing up in the early 1500s with their radical ideas about reform . . . and things were about to change again.

THE REFORMERS

If you're going to have a Reformation, the first thing you need is something to *reform*. And just as important as having something to reform, you need something to reform it *to*. In the case of the Reformers, the object they wanted to reform was the Roman Catholic Church which, as I just said, held a religious monopoly in most of Europe at the time. And the *something* they wanted to reform it *to* was the church found on the pages of the New

Testament. The Reformation, then, was largely a movement to recover Bible doctrine and move things closer to the simplicity and purity of New Testament times.

From the earliest days of the Reformation, one of the doctrinal corruptions that most Reformers cried out against was the corruption of public worship, and one part of that corruption was the use of instruments. One of those Reformers was Huldreich Zwingli, a man some have dubbed the "third man of the Reformation" (behind Martin Luther and John Calvin). Hopefully you recognize Zwingli's name from our baptism discussion in chapter 2. Timothy George, a professor of history and doctrine at the Beeson Divinity School, gives us a good feel for just how passionate Zwingli was about getting rid of instruments in worship:

> The Catholic authorities were shocked at the rigor with which Zwingli pursued his reforms . . . In 1527 the organ at the Great Minster was dismantled and removed, despite the fact that Zwingli was an accomplished musician who had mastered a number of instruments.[8]

John Calvin was equally passionate in his disdain for instruments in worship, and equally rigorous in his pursuit of banishing them from the church assembly. Here's his view which pretty-well represents the thinking of most of his fellow Reformers:

> I have no doubt that playing upon cymbals, touching the harp and the viol, and all that kind of music, which is so frequently mentioned in the Psalms, was part of the . . . service of the Temple. . . . but when they [Christians] frequent their sacred assemblies, musical instruments in celebrating the praises of God would be no more suitable than

the burning of incense, the lighting up of lamps, and the restoration of the other shadows of the law [the Law of Moses]. The Papists [Catholics], therefore, have foolishly borrowed this, as well as many other things from the Jews. Men who are fond of outward pomp may delight in that noise; but the simplicity which God recommends to us by the apostle is far more pleasing to him[9]

Here's another statement by Calvin which makes his no-instruments-in-worship view equally clear:

To sing the praises of God upon the harp and psaltery unquestionably formed part of the training of the law [the Law of Moses], and of the service of God under that dispensation of shadows and figures [the Old Testament period]; but they are not now to be used in public thanksgiving. We are not, indeed, forbidden to use, in private, musical instruments, but they are banished out of the churches by the plain command of the Holy Spirit, when Paul, in 1 Cor. 14:13, lays it down as an invariable rule, that we must praise God, and pray to him only in a known tongue.[10]

Perhaps John Price best sums up the attitude of most Reformers when he says, "The Protestant Reformers showed unrelenting zeal to remove the idolatrous practices introduced by the Roman Catholic Church, including its use of musical instruments . . . So passionate were they against their use, that one reformer said of the organ, 'There's a demon in every pipe.'"[11] Price also sums up well their success in having instruments booted from worship:

They would take no rest until instruments were removed . . . By the late 1500s, this corruption of church worship, which had crept in during the dark ages, had been effectively banished from the Reformed churches. The greatest spiritual revival since the days of the apostles had returned the church to the apostolic simplicity of unaccompanied congregational singing.[12]

THE PURITANS

As the 1600s rolled around, the Puritans, both American and English, continued to hold the same view of instruments in worship that most of the Reformers held. Take a look at what the late historian and former Harvard professor Henry Wilder Foote wrote:

> The Puritans were not, of course, peculiar in their disapproval of instrumental music in church. They could quote Tertullian, Clement of Alexandria, St. Chrysostom, St. Ambrose, St. Augustine, St. Jerome, and others of the early Church Fathers in support of their opinion.[13]

Another prominent church historian, long-time Princeton professor Horton Davies, made this observation about the Puritans:

> The Puritans welcomed instrumental music into their homes while refusing its assistance in their meetinghouses. This restriction is based, in part, on the demand for simplicity and sincerity in worship, but also on their interpretation of Scripture and the finality of the authority of the New Testament for them . . .[14]

Now watch how Davies summarized the thinking of the early American Puritans: "It was not that they disliked music, but that they loved the religion of Christ's ordinances more."[15] I absolutely *love* that statement—the Puritans didn't reject instruments in worship because they didn't like instruments, but because they loved following God's will more, and they were convinced that vocal-only praise was His will when they gathered for worship.

THEN IT HAPPENED

That brings us to the 1700s . . . and things are about to change yet again. This is when Christianity's historic vocal-only conviction began to gradually erode among Protestants, and, to make a long story short, by the late 1800s, vocal-only praise was an endangered species in both American and Western European church life. Here's what John Spencer Curwen, a member of the Royal Academy of Music and president of a musical college in London, wrote in 1880: "Men still living can remember the time when organs were very seldom found outside the Church of England. The Methodists, Independents, and Baptists rarely had them, and by Presbyterians they were stoutly opposed."[16]

Remember me telling you that the organ in Zwingli's church—the Great Minster in Zurich—was dismantled and removed in 1527? It was restored in 1874.[17] Like I said, by the late 1800s *a cappella*-only worship had all but disappeared from church life in America and Western Europe.

A lot of my Baptist friends don't know this, but their ancestors were among the last to wave the white flag and surrender to the growing pressure to bring instruments into their services. According to David Benedict, a nineteenth century New England Baptist preacher and historian, the first organ used in Baptist worship was in Pawtucket, Rhode Island about 1820. Forty years later he wrote:

The changes which have been experienced in the feelings of a large portion of our people has often surprised me. Staunch old Baptists in former times would as soon have tolerated the Pope of Rome in their pulpits as an organ in their galleries, and yet the instrument has gradually found its way among them....[18]

It's important to note, however, that even in the late 1800s there were still prominent voices pleading with churches and churchgoers to maintain the historic Christian practice of vocal-only praise. One of those voices belonged to arguably the most loved and most influential Baptist preacher that ever lived—Charles Spurgeon. Although Spurgeon died well over a century ago—1892 to be exact—his books and sermons are still cherished and widely circulated today.

For the last thirty-eight years of his life, Spurgeon filled the pulpit of the largest Baptist Church in the world, the Metropolitan Baptist Tabernacle in London. Every week thousands would flock to central London and sit spellbound as the sound of eloquent preaching reverberated through the largest church building of its day. However, one sound that never reverberated through that building as long as Spurgeon was there was the sound of an instrument during worship. To quote John MacArthur Jr., the popular evangelical preacher and author, "Spurgeon himself would not appreciate our organ."[19] He's right. Spurgeon loathed the idea of worshiping God with instruments as you can see from this statement in his commentary on the Psalms:

David appears to have had a peculiarly tender remembrance of the singing of the pilgrims and assuredly it is the most delightful part of worship and that which comes nearest to the adoration of heaven. What a degradation to supplant the intelligent song of the whole congregation by the theatrical prettinesses of a quartet, the refined niceties of a choir, or the blowing off of wind from inanimate bellows and pipes! We might as well pray by machinery as praise by it.[20]

There you have it—the CliffsNotes-version of the predominantly non-instrumental history of Christian worship. While our commitment to vocal-only praise may make us look like a strange breed of Christian to a lot of modern churchgoers, this super-short history lesson proves that we're anything but strange. Or at least it proves that the vast majority of Christians from the time of the apostles until the nineteenth century were just as strange as we are. Frankly, I feel good about being in that kind of company.

WE'RE STILL NOT ALONE

Although instrumental praise is obviously now the norm among most church groups, I think it's important to point out that we're still not alone in our commitment to unaccompanied singing in worship. There's actually a sizeable chunk of the larger, worldwide Christian community that shares our vocal-only conviction. Most of that chunk—but not all of it—is found in the Orthodox family of churches.

In case you're not too familiar with Orthodox churches, let me shed a little light on them for you. When describing the Christian world, sources will tell you that there are three major Christian traditions—Roman Catholic, Protestant, and Orthodox. I know you've heard of the first two because those are the categories that most Americans put themselves in if they claim to be a Christian. The reason few Americans identify themselves as Orthodox is because most Orthodox churches are found in Greece, Russia, Ukraine, Romania and other Eastern European and Mediterranean countries. I wouldn't necessarily say that Orthodox churches are extremely rare in the United States—you can find at least one in most mid-sized cities—but I would definitely describe them as being few and far between.

The Orthodox tradition popped up almost a thousand years ago (around the year 1054) as the result of a formal split between the western and eastern parts of the Catholic empire. Historians call this split "the East-West Schism" or "the Great Schism." To make another long story short, the western part of that empire later became known as the Roman Catholic Church while the eastern part became the Eastern Orthodox Church. Since that time, Catholicism has continued to be the dominant Christian tradition in the West while Orthodoxy is still the dominant tradition in the East.

As far as the numbers go, most estimates I've seen put the number of Orthodox adherents in the neighborhood of 250 million worldwide. For comparison, a little over a billion people claim to be Catholic, and roughly 500 million would call themselves Protestant.

Now back to the matter of vocal-only praise. After "the Great Schism," *a cappella*-only worship was the practice in both Catholic and Orthodox churches. But as instruments began to creep into Roman Catholic worship in the 1300s, Orthodox churches remained firmly committed to non-instrumental praise. Today, seven hundred years later, they're still committed to vocal-only worship.

THE "WHY?" QUESTION

Now that you know Christian worship was instrument-free for most of its history, it's time to answer the "Why?" question. Why did most Christians throughout history practice vocal-only praise when they gathered for worship? And why do we in churches of Christ still do so?

The answer begins with a firm conviction that God is in charge of every element of worship, *including the use of instruments in worship*. What exactly does that mean? It means we believe God alone has the authority to decide whether or not to use instruments in worship. If He hasn't placed any instruments in His worship, we don't believe we have the authority to bring any in.

Now let me take you on a short walk through the Bible so you can see how we, and most Christians throughout history, came to this conclusion. We'll begin our walk in the Old Testament in the days of Moses, and in the days when the tabernacle was the center of public worship for God's people.

OLD TESTAMENT TABERNACLE WORSHIP

Soon after giving birth to the nation of Israel through the extraordinary exodus-from-Egypt episode, God drafted and delivered legislation to deal with virtually every aspect of their national life, including worship. In His legislation for worship, God regulated everything from the specs for building the tabernacle and its furnishings, to the clothing and responsibilities of the priests, to the sacrifices which were to be offered, *to the instruments which were to be played.*

When it came to the use of instruments in tabernacle worship, God specifically told Moses what instruments to use, who could use them, and when they were to be used. Take a look:

> The LORD spoke to Moses, saying, **"Make two silver trumpets.** Of hammered work you shall make them, and you shall use them for summoning the congregation and for breaking camp . . . And **the sons of Aaron, the priests, shall blow the trumpets** . . . On the day of your gladness also, and at your appointed feasts and at the beginnings of your months, **you shall blow the trumpets over your burnt offerings and over the sacrifices of your peace offerings.** They shall be a reminder of you before your God: I am the LORD your God" (Numbers 10:1-2, 8, 10).

These instructions seem to make it clear that the use of instruments in tabernacle worship was God's call, and His alone. I can't imagine anyone arguing that Moses was free to add other instruments to the two trumpets that God specifically commanded. Nor can I imagine anyone saying that Moses had the authority to get rid of those trumpets. Although Moses was God's right-hand man, and his relationship with God came with privileges that no other person had, he still didn't have the freedom to change any element of God's plan for tabernacle worship, including His plan for the use of instruments.

OLD TESTAMENT TEMPLE WORSHIP

Years later, when God's people were firmly settled in the

Promised Land, and the ark of the covenant was permanently parked in their capital city of Jerusalem, the center of public worship moved from the tabernacle to the temple. This transition took place under David's oversight (around 1,000 B.C.), and he made some distinct changes to God's worship. One of those changes was the addition of several new instruments. Notice what 1 Chronicles 16:4-6 says:

> Then he [David] *appointed some of the Levites as ministers before the ark of the LORD, to invoke, to thank, and to praise the LORD*, the God of Israel. Asaph was the chief, and second to him were Zechariah, Jeiel, Shemiramoth, Jehiel, Mattithiah, Eliab, Benaiah, Obed-edom, and Jeiel, who were *to play harps and lyres*; Asaph was *to sound the cymbals*, and Benaiah and Jahaziel the priests were *to blow trumpets regularly before the ark of the covenant of God.*

And here's what you'll read a few chapters later:

> When David was old and full of days, he made Solomon his son king over Israel. David assembled all the leaders of Israel and the priests and the Levites. The Levites, thirty years old and upward, were numbered, and the total was 38,000 men. "Twenty-four thousand of these," *David said*, "shall have charge of the work in the house of the LORD, 6,000 shall be officers and judges, 4,000 gatekeepers, and *4,000 shall offer praises to the LORD with the instruments that I have made for praise*" (1 Chronicles 23:1-5).

As we learned a minute ago, in tabernacle worship there were only two silver trumpets which would be blown during certain sacrificial offerings. But now David comes along and adds harps, lyres, and cymbals to the mix in temple worship. The big question is, "Why did David do this?"

Was it because he just wasn't a big fan of trumpet-only music and so he decided to add some musical variety in hopes that it would enhance his own worship experience? Not quite. Maybe he did it because he thought some new instruments would enhance the worship experience of his fellow temple goers. That's not it either. Perhaps he was just knuckling under to the temple goers of his day who were demanding a bigger, better worship band. Hardly.

We discover the real answer when we fast-forward almost three hundred years to the reign of Hezekiah. 2 Chronicles 29 records how Hezekiah restored temple worship after a long period of decay and neglect, and it spells out the reason David brought new instruments into God's worship: "And he [Hezekiah] stationed the Levites in the house of the LORD with cymbals, harps, and lyres, *according to the commandment of David . . . for the commandment was from the LORD through his prophets*. (2 Chronicles 29:25).

There it is. The reason David brought new instruments into temple worship was because God commanded him to bring them in. David's commands for which instruments to use in temple worship were God's commands, just as Moses's commands for which instruments to use in tabernacle worship were God's commands. David himself made this clear when he handed over the detailed plans for the temple and its services to his son Solomon:

> *Then David gave Solomon his son the plan* of the vestibule of the temple, and of its houses, its treasuries, its upper rooms, and its inner chambers, and of the room for the mercy seat; and the plan of all that he had in mind for the courts of the house of the LORD, all the surround-

> ing chambers, the treasuries of the house of God, and the treasuries for dedicated gifts; *for the divisions of the priests and of the Levites, and all the work of the service in the house of the LORD;* . . . *"All this he made clear to me in writing from the hand of the LORD,* all the work to be done according to the plan" (1 Chronicles 28:11-13, 19).

Did you see it? David said he received every detail of temple worship "from the hand of the Lord." Since David added new instruments to temple worship only because God commanded it, doesn't it seem obvious that only God had the authority to add those instruments? If that doesn't seem obvious to you yet, let me show you a few more passages that I think will convince you that no human being had the freedom to change any detail of temple worship, including which instruments were to be used.

We took a look at the first part of this passage just a second ago, but I want us to re-visit a slightly expanded reading of it. Again, it describes King Hezekiah's temple reforms nearly three hundred years after God first revealed His plans for temple worship to David:

> *And he* [Hezekiah] *stationed the Levites in the house of the LORD with cymbals, harps, and lyres, according to the commandment of David . . . for the commandment was from the LORD through his prophets.* The Levites stood *with the instruments of David,* and the priests with the trumpets. Then Hezekiah commanded that the burnt offering be offered on the altar. And when the burnt offering began, the song to the LORD began also, and the trumpets, *accompanied by the instruments of David king of Israel.* The whole assembly worshiped, and the singers sang, and the trumpeters sounded. All this continued until the burnt offering was finished. When the offering was finished, the king and all who were

present with him bowed themselves and worshiped (2 Chronicles 29: 25-29).

Think about what you just read, especially the parts I highlighted. When Hezekiah set out to restore temple worship almost three centuries after David died, he pulled out David's instructions to see which instruments to use. And he only used the instruments which were "according to the commandment of David," or to put it another way, he only used "the instruments of David."

When it came to instruments in temple worship, apparently Hezekiah wasn't the least bit concerned about his own musical tastes or the musical tastes of the people. He was only concerned with "the commandment of David." Why? Because he knew "the commandment of David" concerning temple instruments was "the commandment . . . from the Lord." Hezekiah obviously accepted the fact that God alone had authority over the use of instruments in worship. And Hezekiah understood that "the instruments of David" were the only instruments that God specifically placed in temple worship.

Now let's jump ahead another two hundred years or so. That brings us to about five hundred years after David, and it brings us to a moment in history when the Israelites were rebuilding the temple after the Babylonians had turned it into a pile of smoldering rubble. The men who were handed the reins of this building program were Zerubbabel and Jeshua. When the foundation of the new temple was laid, Ezra gave this report from the scene:

> And when the builders laid the foundation of the temple of the LORD, the priests in their vestments came forward *with trumpets*, and the Levites, the sons of Asaph, *with cymbals, to praise the LORD, according to the directions of David king of Israel* (Ezra 3:10).

That sounds familiar, doesn't it? When Zerubbabel and Jeshua reinstituted temple worship, their approach was exactly the same as Hezekiah's some two hundred years earlier—they did everything, including choosing the instruments, "according to the directions of David king of Israel." Like Hezekiah some two centuries earlier, they obviously accepted the fact that God alone had authority over the use of instruments in worship. And like Hezekiah, they obviously accepted the fact that God revealed His plan for instruments in temple worship through David.

Let's hit fast-forward one more time and stop about fifty years later. Now nearly 550 years have been chalked off the calendar since God first revealed His plans for temple worship to David. And now, once again, those plans need to be restored among His people. This time God taps a man named Nehemiah on the shoulder and commissions him to lead the restoration, and here's what part of that restoration looked like:

> The heads of the Levites were Hashabiah, Sherebiah and Jeshua . . . to praise and give thanks, *as prescribed by David the man of God*, division corresponding to division . . . and some of the sons of the priests with trumpets . . . *with the musical instruments of David the man of God*. . . . For they performed the worship of their God and the service of purification . . . *in accordance with the command of David* . . . (Nehemiah 12:24, 35-36, 45).

Isn't that amazing? When it was Nehemiah's turn to restore temple worship, his plan mirrored both Hezekiah's plan and Zerubbabel's plan. That plan was to do everything "as prescribed by David the man of God." When it came time to decide which instruments to use, Nehemiah didn't stray from that plan. He didn't look to contemporary culture or his own personal tastes for making that decision. He only used "the musical instruments of David the man of God." Nehemiah made sure that every element of temple worship, including the use of instruments, was "in accordance with the command of David."

Nehemiah obviously understood the same thing that Hezekiah and Zerubbabel understood when it came to the use of instruments in God's worship. He understood that instruments were under God's authority alone, which meant that he didn't have the freedom to add or take away any instrument from the plan that God gave David. And now we come to worship in the New Testament age.

NEW TESTAMENT CHRISTIAN WORSHIP

When it came to deciding whether or not to use instruments in Christian worship, most believers from the time of the apostles until the nineteenth century found nothing in the New Testament to suggest that God had delegated that decision to His people. As a result, most Christians throughout history applied the lesson they learned from Old Testament worshipers like Hezekiah, Zerubbabel, and Nehemiah.

That lesson was to consult the instructions of those to whom God revealed His plans for worship, and then precisely follow those instructions without adding or subtracting anything. But while tabernacle worshipers consulted the instructions of Moses, and temple worshipers—like Hezekiah, Zerubbabel, and Nehemiah—consulted the instructions of David, Christian worshipers consulted the instructions of the apostles.

Why the change? Why did Christians consult the apostles for direction in worship instead of Moses or David? Simply put, because the Old Testament, along with its temple system of worship, was permanently shelved when Jesus died on the cross. In its place, God began delivering His new covenant through His apostles on the Day of Pentecost.

In this New Testament system, God dramatically changed how His people would worship Him, and He revealed His new plans for worship through His apostles. That's why the early church "devoted themselves to the apostles' teaching" (Acts 2:42) instead of David's or Moses's teaching.

You can see a good example of the apostles exercising their God-given authority over Christian worship when Paul takes control of an out-of-control church assembly in Corinth. When he first wrote to them, he put a stop to their chaos by establishing clear rules for speaking in the assembly (1 Corinthians 14:26-36). He then punctuated those rules with this: "If anyone thinks that he is a prophet, or spiritual, he should acknowledge that *the things I am writing to you are a command of the Lord.* If anyone does not recognize this, he is not recognized" (1 Corinthians 14:37-38). Obviously, the Corinthians weren't free to keep doing their own thing. Obviously, God expected them to follow Paul's orders.

Since God revealed His plans for Christian worship through

His apostles, when it came to the question of whether or not to use instruments, most believers throughout history simply asked, "What instruments do the apostles command us to use?" And the answer always came back the same—none.

As the Church Fathers and Reformers and Puritans scoured the pages of the New Testament they found commands to *sing* praise to God (Ephesians 5:19; Colossians 3:16; James 5:13), and they found examples of believers praising Him in song (Acts 16:25; 1 Corinthians 14:15), but they couldn't find even a hint of an instrument in worship. LaGard Smith was right when he wrote:

> In contrast to the many Old Testament passages referring to musical instruments in temple worship, in the New Testament text not one sound of a musical instrument is heard—not a trumpet, not a harp, not the quietest jingle of a tambourine! Singing, yes. Musical instruments, no. Relative to musical instruments, there is only an ominous haunting silence.[21]

Even those who worship with instruments will admit that their practice is nowhere to be found in the New Testament if they're totally objective with the facts. For instance, Robert Godfrey—he's the seminary president and church history professor I quoted earlier—put it this way: "Nowhere in the New Testament church are instruments clearly used for worship."[22] I really appreciate that kind of honesty.

For most Christians throughout history, all these things added up to a simple conclusion—*since God didn't place any instruments in Christian worship, they weren't going to bring any in.*

For most of us in churches of Christ, we believe this historic

Christian approach to instruments in worship is theologically sound. Here's a quick summary:

- In the Old Testament, God alone had authority over the use of instruments in both tabernacle and temple worship.

- God specifically placed certain instruments in both tabernacle and temple worship, and no person had the authority to add or take away from the instruments He placed there.

- As God inaugurated His new covenant, there's nothing in the New Testament to suggest that He gave up His authority over the use of instruments in worship.

- If God wanted instruments in Christian worship, it's reasonable to conclude that He would have specifically placed them there through His apostles, just as He did in tabernacle worship through Moses and in temple worship through David.

- There isn't a single command from the apostles to use instruments in Christian worship, nor a single example in the New Testament of Christians worshiping with instruments.

For us, these things add up to the same simple conclusion that the vast majority of our Christian ancestors came to, and that means we're going to continue to stand where they stood—*since God didn't place any instruments in Christian worship, we aren't going to bring any in.*

A MODERN RESTORATION STORY

When I think about the concept of restoration—restoring the beliefs and practices of the church in New Testament times—I immediately think of a book that hit the shelves in 2005 called *Old Light On New Worship*.[23] As a lifelong singer of vocal-only praise in church, it was actually the subtitle that caught my eye: *Musical Instruments and the Worship of God, a Theological, Historical and Psychological Study*. But while the subtitle caught my eye, it was the author that really piqued my curiosity—John Price, a Reformed Baptist minister from New York.

In the preface, Price explained how the book came into being. First, though, you need to know that Reformed Baptist churches have almost always used only one instrument to accompany their congregational singing, usually a piano. I'll let Price take it from here:

> More than three years ago, a study was conducted in a sister Reformed Baptist church with the conclusion that various musical instruments are warranted in New Testament worship. The audio tapes of this study came into the possession of one of the members of my congregation who then passed them on to me. I later became aware that these tapes were having a wider distribution with some influence among other Reformed Baptists. In listening to those tapes, I realized that further study was necessary on this subject. What began as a relatively brief study developed over time into this book.[24]

After presenting the fruits of his exhaustive study to the congregation, they came to a conclusion. Remember, the choices were: (1) remain committed to their historic use of only one instrument in worship, or (2) acknowledge that multiple instruments in worship are permissible. They chose neither. Instead, here's what happened: "As a result of this study . . . We have become convinced that we should no longer use any musical instrument in accompanying our congregational singing."[25]

Pretty interesting, wouldn't you say? It reminds me of the people in Nehemiah's day after they discovered the long-lost hut-building command of God (Nehemiah 8:13-17). As I said in chapter 1, they were so committed to obeying God that they said, in effect, "Wow, we're supposed to be sitting around in huts while observing this feast. Let's go get these huts built!" In that same spirit, this Reformed Baptist church said, in effect, "Wow, we shouldn't be using any instruments while offering our praise to God. Let's get rid of our piano!"

My prayer is that more and more Bible-believers will embrace that same spirit of restoration in worship and choose to go back to the simple New Testament practice of vocal-only praise. Granted, that would be a startling, radical change. But restoration usually is startling and radical. That's why true restoration demands boldness. May we all have the boldness to follow the will of God, no matter what.

CHAPTER 4

THE LORD'S DAY & THE LORD'S SUPPER IN THE SHAPE OF THE NEW TESTAMENT

As the countdown to the cross was nearing zero, Jesus had one more very important detail to take care of before He allowed Himself to be cuffed and led away to His divinely orchestrated destiny. That important detail was the establishment of a practice that would be a central activity in the weekly assembly of every future congregation of His people. So during Passover, while sequestered with His disciples in an upper room somewhere among the maze of Jerusalem's narrow streets, Jesus took some unleavened bread (bread without yeast) and fruit of the vine (some form of grape juice), and He instituted the Lord's Supper (Matthew 26:26-29; Mark 14:22-25; Luke 22:14-23; 1 Corinthians 11:23-26).

If you visit a church of Christ this coming Sunday, I can assure you that partaking of unleavened bread and fruit of the vine will be one of the activities you'll encounter during the service. And if you attend that same church of Christ the following Sunday, I guarantee a replay of the Lord's Supper. And if you attend the Sunday service of that very same church of Christ eight weeks later, or eight months later, or eight years later, I promise the Lord's Supper will be a central part of each of those Sunday services.

I think you get the point, and the point is, we take the Lord's Supper *every* Sunday . . . and, I might add, *only* every Sunday. This practice has always been a very important part of our doctrinal identity, and it's another very important difference between us and most other church groups.

Unlike churches of Christ, most Protestant and evangelical churches usually partake of the Lord's Supper at less-than-weekly intervals. Some partake once a month, others every three or four months, and still others may only see the Lord's Supper a couple of times a year. In fact, if you were to ask ten people who claim to be Protestant or evangelical how often they observe the Lord's Supper, don't be surprised if you get ten different answers. That's not an exaggeration—it's simply a fact that the frequency of observing the Lord's Supper is all over the board in both the Protestant and evangelical church communities.

BECAUSE THAT'S THE PATTERN

Several years ago I ran across an interesting interview with the late George Beasley-Murray, a man whose name and work is still revered in the world of biblical scholarship. One of the things I found interesting about this scholar who was British by birth and Baptist by faith was that a few of his views aren't typically held by most of my Baptist friends in the United States. Two of those views were the subject of this particular interview: baptism and the Lord's Supper.

While most of my Baptist friends don't partake of the Lord's Supper every Sunday—although I'm thrilled to report that a few have begun to do so in recent years—when Beasley-Murray was asked his view, he said, "My own views as a young pastor speedily led me to the conviction that the primitive New Testament pattern of the weekly observance was there and that there was every reason to follow it."[1]

I, for one, love that statement for several reasons. For one thing, he admitted what some people are reluctant to admit—that there really is a "pattern" of beliefs and practices that churches in the New Testament followed. I also love his acknowledgment that eating the Lord's Supper every week was part of that "primitive New Testament pattern." And finally, I love his conclusion that we should be following that pattern too.

As you know, that's been my mantra throughout this book—we in churches of Christ believe the New Testament contains a pattern that every congregation should still follow, and we're totally committed to trying to do just that. And now you know that we believe eating the Lord's Supper every Sunday is an important part of that pattern.

Now let's take a closer look at the New Testament marriage of the Lord's Day—that is, Sunday—and the Lord's Supper. First, I want to show you that meeting together every Sunday is part of "the primitive New Testament pattern" (to borrow Beasley-Murray's words). After that, I want you to see that partaking of the Lord's Supper during those Sunday gatherings is also part of that pattern.

SUNDAY MEETINGS

When it comes to the activities of the earliest Christians, there are a lot of details we just can't pin down. But one thing we do know for sure is they met together regularly. Here's a sampler of passages which show that meeting together was a regular part of church life in the New Testament: "For a whole year they met with the church . . ." (Acts 11:26); "And when they arrived and gathered the church together . . . (Acts 14:27); "When you are assembled in the name of the Lord . . ." (1 Corinthians 5:4); ". . . when you come together as a church . . ." (1 Corinthians 11:18); and "If, therefore, the whole church comes together . . ." (1 Corinthians 14:23).

If you're inclined to think those meetings were nice-but-not-really-necessary-get-togethers, think again. The New Testament actually teaches that assembling together is an ongoing commitment that God expects every one of His people to keep, hence this reminder by the Holy Spirit: "And let us consider how to stir up one another to love and good works, *not neglecting to meet together, as is the habit of some*, but encouraging one another, and all the more as you see the Day drawing near" (Hebrews 10:24-25).

Apparently truancy from church isn't just a contemporary problem. Of course, without cars, malls, the internet, big-time professional sports, monster TVs with a gazillion channels, and weekend little league baseball and soccer tournaments, I can't imagine what would have kept first-century believers away from their church meetings. I guess every generation and culture has plenty of distractions, both trivial and not-so-trivial, competing for people's hearts and minds.

Anyway, those who say, "I don't have to go to church to be a Christian" are simply resisting God's will, and that reminds me of something I encountered a long time ago that made my head spin, and still makes it spin when I think about it.

I was about twenty-three years old with a freshly minted B.A. in Bible, and my first full-time preaching job, when I decided to start the next phase of my education at a nearby evangelical seminary. It was my first educational experience in the field of theology at a school that wasn't affiliated with churches of Christ, so I knew I'd be encountering some different perspectives, especially since this school was hard-core Calvinistic and I'm not a Calvinist.[2] Still, I never imagined encountering a perspective quite as different as one expressed by a professor when he responded to a classmate's report of a personal evangelism experience.

Just before class began, this young grad student excitedly shared news about a one-on-one Bible study he had the previous night. His report climaxed with the announcement that his student had decided to follow Christ. The professor's first response was a spontaneous expression of praise. His second was a question that I had never heard before, and will never forget—"Is she going to be a church-going Christian?"

I don't really remember what the guy's response was because I was too busy sitting there, head spinning, thinking, "A *what*? A *church-going* Christian? I never knew there was any other kind!"

You see, I was always taught that God was just as serious about His command not to neglect church meetings (Hebrews 10:25) as He was about His commands not to do things like lie (Ephesians 4:25), steal (Ephesians 4:28), or live sexually immoral lives (1 Thessalonians 4:3). And so, I grew up being told that God expects us to be present when the church meets—unless, of course, we're "providentially hindered" (that's how I always heard it put when I was growing up), and we all knew that "providentially hindered" meant you were sick, or had to work, or something like that.

I've thrown away some twenty-three annual calendars since that day in class, and during that time I've done quite a bit of Bible study as I've continued my formal theological education and prepared over twenty-three years worth of sermons and Bible classes. After all that time and Bible study, I'm as convinced as ever that it's patently unbiblical to teach that a person can be a faithful Christian and simply choose not to "go to church."

Assembling together is a very important part of the true church's identity. Our faith is private, or individual, in the sense that no one can believe for us. However, being a faithful Christian definitely requires having a relationship with a group of fellow Christians, and God definitely requires that group—that church—to regularly meet together to worship Him, and build each other up in the faith.

Assuming regular church meetings are part of God's plan to help our faith grow and survive, when and how often should the church meet?

At a minimum, the New Testament points to one particular day for those regular meetings. That day, to use the most common terminology in the New Testament, is "the first day of the week." To use our terminology, it's Sunday.[3] I already gave you a sound-bite—way back in chapter 1—of the emphasis that the New Testament places on Sunday church assemblies. Now I want us take a little more expanded and lingering look at that emphasis.

The New Testament evidence for Sunday assemblies begins in Acts 20 when Paul was coming down the homestretch of his third missionary journey. After he and his missionary team boarded a ship in Philippi (in modern Greece) with their sights set on Jerusalem, they decided to make a pit stop in Troas, a city located on the far northwestern coast of modern-day Turkey. Here's how Luke begins his report of their layover: *"On the first day of the week, when we were gathered together* to break bread, Paul talked with them, intending to depart on the next day, and he prolonged his speech until midnight" (Acts 20:7).

Based on Luke's matter-of-fact way of saying that they gathered with the church on Sunday, it sure sounds like Sunday meetings were a regular practice of the Troas congregation. Of course, some may read that verse and be tempted to say, "Wait a minute. That doesn't necessarily mean Sunday was a regular meeting day for them. Maybe they called a special meeting just because Paul was in town; and maybe they chose that particular day because it just happened to be the day that accommodated the schedule of most members."

Well . . . no. The New Testament provides enough other information for us to confidently say that the church in Troas regularly met on Sunday. That information comes from Paul as he was winding down his first letter to the Corinthian church:

> Now concerning the collection for the saints: as I directed the churches of Galatia, so you also are to do. *On the first day of every week*, each of you is to put something aside and store it up, as he may prosper, so that there will be no collecting when I come (1 Corinthians 16:1-2).

The fact that Paul told this congregation to make a financial contribution "on the first day of every week" seems to clearly imply they were meeting together on that day. Of course since Paul doesn't actually say anything about meeting together, some people aren't ready to admit that his instructions imply a meeting. Apparently some folks are open to the possibility that Paul may have been telling each member to slip some money under their mattress at home, or maybe stick it in a cookie jar, on the first day of every week.

If you think that interpretation sounds plausible, let me ask you this question: What possible sense would it make for Paul to tell people to squirrel away some money at home on a specific day each week? What difference would it make if they stuck some money in an envelope and tucked it in a kitchen drawer on Thursday, or any other day of the week, instead of Sunday? The fact is, Paul's instructions only make sense if there was something about "the first day of every week" that gave them a special opportunity to "put something aside."

What was it about the first day of every week that made it

the perfect opportunity for the Corinthians to make a financial offering? The only reasonable answer is they were meeting together on that day. Sunday meetings gave them the perfect opportunity to collect their money as a congregation.

And it wasn't just the Corinthian church that was meeting on the first day of every week. Notice that Paul's put-something-aside-on-the-first-day-of-every-week order was also given to the churches of Galatia (1 Corinthians 16:1). Obviously, then, every church in every city in the province of Galatia was also meeting on the first day of every week.

If you do a quick check of a Bible atlas, you'll see that, as I've already pointed out, the city of Troas is on the far northwestern coast of modern Turkey, the city of Corinth is in modern-day Greece, and the region of Galatia is in the middle of modern Turkey. That adds up to the realization that these churches weren't exactly close neighbors. In fact, with hundreds of miles between them, they weren't really neighbors at all, at least not in any real geographical sense. And yet all of these congregations assembled on the very same day—the first day of every week.

As I said in chapter 1, that's either an unplanned coincidence or a God-instituted pattern. Quite frankly, I don't know any who have put their money on the "unplanned coincidence" option.

Here's something else I think is pretty interesting. When you understand that Sunday meetings were instituted by God, it would seem to explain a small detail that Luke mentioned as soon as Paul was looking at Troas in his rearview mirror in Acts 20. That small detail was that Paul was in a hurry. Here's how Luke put it: "For Paul had decided to sail past Ephesus, so that he might not have to spend time in Asia, for he was hastening to be at Jerusalem, if possible, on the day of Pentecost" (Acts 20:16).

Now let's jump back to the day that Paul and his team docked in Troas. Luke wrote, "We stayed for seven days" (Acts 20:6). In other words, they pulled into Troas on Monday, and then pulled out immediately after church the next Sunday (Acts 20:11). Here's something to think about—if Paul was in such a rush to get back to Jerusalem, why did he hang around Troas for seven days?

Some have suggested that the long layover may have been due to the ship's schedule. In other words, maybe they were forced to stay there because they had to wait seven days for a ship. Well, maybe. And maybe a ship just happened to become available right after the closing prayer at church on Sunday. If that's the case, I guess Paul couldn't have asked for more perfect timing. Most, however, think there's a better explanation than shipping schedules. That better explanation is worship schedules.

The fact that Luke clocked Paul's sermon as lasting until midnight (Acts 20:17), and then added that Paul talked with the members until daybreak (Acts 20:11), suggests that this stop was driven by Paul's intense desire to meet with the whole church so that he could strengthen and encourage them with the Word of God. To do that, however, Paul had no choice but to wait until "the first day of the week" because that was their regular day of assembly.

Some may wonder why the church didn't just call a special meeting—say, on Tuesday—to accommodate Paul's fast-ticking travel clock. While something like that would certainly be a viable option in our culture, it really wasn't in theirs. So, again, if Paul wanted to encourage the whole church, he really had no choice but to patiently wait for Sunday even though he was pressed for time. Of course that doesn't mean he and his team laid around in hammocks for seven days. I haven't the slightest doubt that they stayed busy evangelizing and ministering among the brethren while they waited for Sunday to roll around (see Acts 21:4).

SUNDAY ASSEMBLY: THE HISTORY TEST

If anyone doubts that Sunday was a regular meeting day for the first generation of God's church, those doubts are erased with a quick check of when the second century church met together.

Before we check that information, though, maybe you're wondering why we should even care about what the second century church did. The answer is, it can help us test our interpretation of what the Bible tells us about the beliefs and practices of the church in New Testament times. How does it do that? Since the second century is the period of history closest to New Testament times, second century Christians are more likely to have shared the same beliefs and practices of Christians in New Testament times.

With that said, one of the best descriptions of when and how second century Christians worshiped comes from a man named Justin Martyr. Around the year 155 he wrote to the Roman emperor Antoninus Pius (AD 138-161) to defend Christianity against charges like immorality and treason. By explaining Christian beliefs and practices to the emperor, Justin hoped the emperor would tolerate Christianity as just another philosophical tradition.

One of the many things that Justin explained to the emperor was the Christian practice of gathering weekly for worship. In that explanation, he pointed out that Sunday was their day of meeting:

> We are always together with one another. And for all the things with which we are supplied we bless the Maker of all through his Son Jesus Christ and through his Holy Spirit. And on the day called Sunday there is a gathering together in the same place of all who live in a city or a rural district. . . . We all make our assembly in common on the day of the Sun . . .[4]

Another important piece of early Christian literature that gives us a glimpse of second century worship is a short document called the *Didache* (pronounced di-dah-KAY), or the "Teaching of the Twelve Apostles."[5] Most scholars think this anonymous document was written sometime between the late first century and early second century, and the purpose was to give Christians some basic instruction on a variety of matters. One of those matters is the requirement to assemble together, and here's how it begins: "Having confessed your sins so that your sacrifice may be pure, come together each Lord's day . . ."[6]

There are a few other references from the second century that I could toss out, but I think these two are sufficient to confirm our interpretation that a Sunday assembly was part of the pattern of church life in the New Testament. And that brings us to a "So what?" moment.

SUNDAY ASSEMBLY: SO WHAT?

If there's one aspect of the New Testament pattern for church life that most churches have historically followed, it's a Sunday assembly. In recent years, however, more and more churches have added a Saturday evening assembly to their line-up of services, and the main reason is to give worshipers an alternative to the traditional church-on-Sunday routine.

Why? Frankly, it's all about accommodating the demands of modern worshipers, and a lot of them simply don't feel like rolling out of bed on Sunday to go to church. For others, there's the Sunday football game, the little league tournament, the golf outing or bike ride with friends, or the day on the lake which they aren't about to pass up for church.

I'm not really surprised that so many of today's churchgoers would opt for church on Saturday night instead of Sunday if given the choice. After all, I probably would if I didn't know better, and a lot contemporary churchgoers simply don't know better because they're functionally illiterate when it comes to basic Bible doctrines. When I say that, I'm not trying to be mean or provocative; I'm just stating the obvious. Social research dealing with matters of faith and religion continue to show that, as I said in the preface, more and more professing Christians see the fundamentals of Christianity as little more than having some kind of belief that Jesus saves, and doing nice things for others—like generously tipping your waiter, making an occasional donation to the charity of your choice, recycling and going green whenever possible, and for the most part trying to follow that do-unto-others rule.

What does surprise me, and troubles me, is that so many church leaders are apparently just as in the dark when it comes to understanding the significance of the Lord's Day and respecting God's plan to meet on that day. Apparently many have concluded that the early church met on Sunday simply because it was a convenient time and not because it was a commanded time.

I'll admit that the percentage of churches offering a Saturday service as an alternative to Sunday is still relatively small, but the number has grown over the last several years. Of course, only time will tell if it becomes a common practice in North American Christianity. I can assure you of one thing, though, and that's this—if Saturday services eventually become a familiar sight in American church culture, it won't become a familiar sight among churches of Christ. I know my brethren pretty well, so I can say with confidence that most of us will continue to follow the practice of our spiritual ancestors in the New Testament, and that means we'll keep calling our members to meet together "on the first day of every week."

Don't get me wrong though. I'm not saying that a church can't meet on Saturday evening. There's plenty of New Testament evidence to show that we can gather for worship and mutual encouragement whenever and wherever we want (Acts 2:46-47; 12:12). What I'm saying is, regardless of how often we choose to meet, at a minimum we must assemble on Sunday.

I would love to start explaining right now why Sunday is so significant in God's plan for His church, but I'm going to resist that urge for a few minutes. Instead, let's turn our attention to the Lord's Supper.

SUNDAY ASSEMBLY: MEETING TO EAT

As we read about the churches in Troas and Corinth, we not only discover that those congregations met together on Sunday, but we also discover that a main purpose of their Sunday meetings was to eat the Lord's Supper.

Back to Acts 20:7: "On the first day of the week, *when we were gathered together to break bread*." Luke gives it to us short and sweet—the Troas church met on Sunday, and a central purpose of that meeting was to take the Lord's Supper, or "to break bread," to stick with his terminology.

What about the church in Corinth? We saw how Paul clearly implied that, like the church in Troas, the Corinthians were meeting together "on the first day of every week" (1 Corinthians 16:1-2). Unlike Luke's statement about Troas, however, Paul didn't specifically say in 1 Corinthians 16 that the Lord's Supper was being eaten in Corinth each Sunday.

If you flip back just a few chapters, though, you'll see that eating the Lord's Supper was supposed to be the main purpose of the church meetings in Corinth too: "So then, my brothers, *when you come together to eat* . . ." (1 Corinthians 11:33). Of course that verse doesn't tell us exactly what they were supposed to be eating when they came together, but we know it's the Lord's Supper because just a few verses earlier Paul rebuked them with these words: "When you come together, it is not the Lord's Supper that you eat" (1 Corinthians 11:20). Paul's point was that they should have been eating the Lord's Supper at their meetings, but they messed it up so badly that it couldn't even be called the Lord's Supper anymore.

Instead of communing together as a unified congregation, many were treating the Lord's Supper like a private potluck to share with just a few close friends. They were not, in Paul's words, "discerning the body" (1 Corinthians 11:29),[7] and the result was a congregation peppered with "divisions" (1 Corinthians 11:18).

Through careful teaching, though, Paul started the process of straightening up the mess they had made of the Lord's Supper. His final written instructions to this divided bunch concerning the Supper was, "So then, my brothers, when you come together to eat, wait for one another—if anyone is hungry, let him eat at home—so that when you come together it will not be for judgment." (1 Corinthians 11:33-34).

As we'll see in a moment, we can learn quite a bit about the *meaning* of the Lord's Supper from 1 Corinthians 11. For now, though, I don't want you to miss the fact that this passage seems to make it clear that the Lord's Supper was to be a central feature of the Sunday assemblies in Corinth just as it was a central feature of the Sunday assemblies in Troas.

SUNDAY LORD'S SUPPER: THE HISTORY TEST

We already saw that churches in the second century met together every Sunday, which lends strong support to our view that Sunday meetings are part of the New Testament pattern for church life. Now let's take another quick look at church life in the second century to see if it supports our view that eating the Lord's Supper every Sunday is also part of God's New Testament pattern for His church.

To make it easy, we'll stick with the two second century

sources we looked at earlier—Justin Martyr's letter to the Roman emperor, and the *Didache*. Let's start with Justin. In case you forgot, he wrote his letter to the emperor around the year 155 hoping to persuade him to tolerate Christianity as just another philosophical tradition. Here's his description of what second century Christians did in their Sunday gatherings:

> And on the day called Sunday there is a gathering together in the same place of all who live in a city or a rural district. The memoirs of the apostles or the writings of the prophets are read, as long as time permits. Then when the reader ceases, the president[8] in a discourse admonishes and urges the imitation of these good things. Next we all rise together and send up prayers. And, as I said before, *when we cease from our prayer, bread is presented with wine and water.* The president in the same manner sends up prayers and thanksgiving according to his ability, and people sing out their assent saying the "Amen." *A distribution and participation of the elements from which thanks have been given is made to each person,* and to those who are not present it is sent by the deacons. Those who have means and are willing, each according to his own choice, gives what he wills, and what is collected is deposited with the president. He provides for the orphans and widows, those who are in want on account of sickness or some other cause, those who are in bonds and strangers who are sojourning, and in a word he becomes the protector of all who are in need.[9]

Although Justin didn't actually use the term "the Lord's Supper," or the expression "break bread," nobody has tried to suggest that his reference to a "distribution and participation" of "bread" and a mixture of "wine and water" is something other than the Lord's Supper, and rightly so.[10]

Now let's go back to the *Didache*, and just in case you forgot what that is, it's a document from the late first century or early second century which gives basic Christian instruction on a variety of matters. As we saw earlier, one of those matters is the requirement to assemble together, and, once again, here's how that instruction begins: "Having confessed your sins so that your sacrifice may be pure, come together each Lord's day . . ."

Thanks to the ellipsis at the end of that quote, you know there's more to that instruction. Here, now, is the rest of it: "Having confessed your sins so that your sacrifice may be pure, come together each Lord's day of the Lord [sic], **break bread**, and give thanks."[11] As you can see, not only were these early Christians told to meet together every Sunday, but they were also told to eat the Lord's Supper—that is, "break bread"—at those meetings.

In my mind that pretty much clinches things. Since the second century church clearly ate the Lord's Supper each Sunday, I'm confident that we in churches of Christ have understood the New Testament correctly when we say, to borrow Beasley-Murray's words again, "the primitive New Testament pattern of the weekly observance" is there, and we should follow it.

THE NOT-SO-SURPRISING CONNECTION

Now it's time to do what I had to resist doing earlier, and that's to remind us why God put Sunday church meetings and eating the Lord's Supper together. There's really no mystery to this marriage, but for some reason the clear biblical significance of Sunday seems to have been lost on many of today's churchgoers, probably because it's not taught much anymore. Let's face it, it's no secret that teaching doctrine has fallen out of favor in many church settings.

What's the big deal about Sunday? Why has God called us together to break bread on that particular day? Because, by God's design, that's the day Jesus finished His saving work by walking out of His tomb alive.

One of the interesting things about the four Gospel writers is they rarely mention the specific day of the week on which events in the life of Jesus took place. And yet, without exception, the Holy Spirit made sure that Matthew, Mark, Luke, and John all announced the specific day of the week that Jesus's tomb was found empty— "the first day of the week" (Matthew 28:1; Mark 16:2; Luke 24:1; John 20:1).

Not only that, John specifically reported that it was on the same "first day of the week" that Jesus met with His apostles and took away their doubts about His resurrection by showing them His wounded hands and side (John 20:19-20). John also made sure we knew it was exactly one week later, the very next Sunday, that Jesus met with them again, this time removing all of Thomas's doubts about His resurrection (John 20:26-28).[12]

Can you see it now? Can you see the connection? Jesus rose from the dead on Sunday, and on that very same day, as well as the very next Sunday—the one week anniversary of His resurrection—Jesus came to His gathered apostles and showed them His crucified body. And now, every Sunday, on the weekly anniversary of His resurrection, Jesus comes to His gathered church and He shows us His crucified body through the bread we eat and the cup we drink; and in doing so He reminds us that He was once dead, but now is alive. It's no wonder Christians started calling Sunday "the Lord's Day" so quickly (see Revelation 1:10).

I think LaGard Smith was absolutely right when he said, "I don't know about you, but this is the stuff of which goose bumps are made."[13] He then added:

> How then, by any means, can professing Christians still ask us whether they have to take the Lord's Supper every week, as opposed to monthly or quarterly? When Jesus said, "whenever you eat this bread and drink this cup . . ." he wasn't telling us to partake of the Supper just whenever, as if whenever we feel like it, or whenever it's convenient. In those inaugural words, Jesus was giving us the meaning of the memorial. It was the Spirit-led, first-century church which demonstrated the mode. By convincing evidence, that mode was weekly. Considering the wonders of its continuous "revelations," who would wish otherwise?[14]

He's right. When Jesus said "whenever you eat this bread and drink this cup," He wasn't telling us to take the Supper whenever we feel like it. And yet "whenever we feel like it" seems to be the primary criteria that most Protestant and evangelical church groups have historically used to decide when to take it. Even some churches that take it every Sunday also feel free to take it on other days of the week or special occasions.[15] It makes me wonder if the incredible significance of the Lord's Day is being lost. Or has it already been lost?

While I certainly respect the sincerity, devotion, and motives of those who believe that anytime-is-the-right-time to take the Lord's Supper, most of us in churches of Christ simply can't endorse that practice. Since the New Testament pattern is to take the Lord's Supper on the Lord's Day, we'll continue to reserve the Lord's Supper for the Lord's Day and the Lord's Day for the Lord's Supper. As I've heard some put it, "No Lord's Day without the Lord's Supper, and no Lord's Supper without the Lord's Day."

THE LORD'S SUPPER: WHAT'S IT ALL ABOUT?

So far I've focused almost exclusively on why we're committed to following the New Testament pattern of eating the Lord's Supper every Lord's Day, and *only* every Lord's Day. Now let me offer a word of caution. While I'm convinced that getting the timing right is a very important feature of the New Testament pattern for the Lord's Supper, let me add that I don't think for one minute that timing is everything.

In our discussions of the Lord's Supper, if we put virtually all our emphasis on eating it on the right day and at the right frequency, we can't really blame people if they start thinking the only thing that matters is getting those two things right. And if that happens, the Lord's Supper can easily wind up becoming a thoughtless Sunday ritual that neither pleases God nor blesses us.

It's important to understand that every activity that God has placed among us is intended to pass along spiritual blessings that will help our faith survive and thrive. The Lord's Supper is no exception. But those blessings don't just automatically ooze over us when we take a communion tray from our pew-neighbor and partake of its contents. We have to pave the way for receiving those blessings, and we do that when we "examine" ourselves as we participate in this simple weekly activity (1 Corinthians 11:28).

I'm fully aware that, in context, Paul's call for self-examination primarily seems to be a call for us to examine our relationship with our spiritual brothers and sisters. I'm convinced, though, that it has a wider application than just that. I believe he's telling us to come to the table contemplating the meaning and significance of what we're about to put into our mouths.

For the next few minutes, let's do just that—let's explore and contemplate what this weekly activity is all about. And I think the best way to do that is to think about some of the terms which are associated with it in the New Testament. By the way, you may want to find a place in your Bible to jot some of these things down. That way, as you come to the table each week, you'll be able flip to these notes if you're feeling the need for some direction in your thinking.

Lord's Supper

Let's start with the term I've been using the most, which also happens to be the most popular term among Protestants and evangelicals—the "Lord's Supper." This term should constantly remind us that, when we're participating in this activity, we're participating in an activity that's uniquely the Lord's.

It's His supper, not ours (1 Corinthians 11:20-21). It's His table, not ours (1 Corinthians 10:21). Jesus sets the table for us, and invites us to join Him. We come to the table each Sunday as His invited guests, and as we eat and drink, we're honoring Him as God's indescribable gift to us.

Thanksgiving

In all four accounts of Christ instituting His supper, the verb "give thanks" is used (Matthew 26:27; Mark 14:23; Luke 22:17; 1 Corinthians 11:24). The Greek word behind that English translation is *eucharisteo*, and that's why you'll hear some people refer to the Lord's Supper as "the Eucharist."

Each time we come to the table and thank God for the bread and cup, it's a reminder that eternal life is something God has freely given to us, and not something we earn or deserve. What's more, it's a reminder that the only reason we've been given eternal life is because God sent Jesus to the cross, and His death somehow paid our penalty of an eternity in hell.

Communion

Paul says the cup we drink is "a *koinonia* (that's the Greek word he uses) in the blood of Christ," and the bread we eat is "a *koinonia* in the body of Christ" (1 Corinthians 10:16-17). In this passage, most English Bibles translate that word "sharing" (NASB, NLT) or "participation" (NIV, ESV). The King James Version, though, translates it "communion." And since the KJV was *the* Bible for generations of English-speaking worshipers, "communion" became a common way of referring to the Lord's Supper.

The basic meaning of *koinonia* is conveyed not only in our English words *sharing*, *participation*, and *communion*, but also in our word *fellowship*. In fact, in most places where *koinonia* appears in the Greek New Testament, it's translated "fellowship" in our English Bibles.

Paul seems to be saying that we are personally *sharing* in Christ's sacrifice and its benefits when we gather at His table to eat and drink. We are personally *participating* in His body and blood. In other words, as we eat and drink, we're saying that our identity has been transformed and shaped by Jesus's death. We're saying that His death has changed us to be like Him. We're saying that, because of His death, we now share a deep, intimate bond with Him, and we're totally committed to Him.

We not only commune with the Lord, though, but also with each other. Paul follows up the *koinonia* verse with these words: "Because there is one bread, we who are many are one body, for we all partake of the one bread" (1 Corinthians 10:17). As we eat the bread and drink the cup, we're proclaiming that we're united in the same family, and that we're committed to one another now and through eternity. This was the point Paul was making as he tried to get the Lord Supper back on the right track in Corinth (1 Corinthians 11:17-34).

There's also another term that's associated with the Lord's Supper which calls our attention to our intimate bond—our fellowship—with each other, and that term is "break bread" (Acts 20:7). That expression conveys the idea of sharing food together, and table fellowship in New Testament culture was something very different than it is in our culture. In the biblical world, sharing food was a sign of extreme closeness. It said volumes about the relationship between participants. With this in mind, as we break bread each Lord's Day, we need to remember that God calls us to extreme closeness with our brothers and sisters in Christ.

Memorial

We're able to have an intimate bond with Jesus and each other because of a past event, and when we eat the Lord's Supper, we're commemorating and remembering that event—the death and resurrection of Christ (1 Corinthians 11:24-25). But we need to remember God's work at the cross the same way Jews remember God's work in the exodus.

When Jews celebrate Passover, they see themselves as actually participating in the exodus. They are individually challenged to think of themselves as being the very one that God brought out of Egypt. In other words, as they remember, they bring the past into the present and think of it in a very personal way.

As we eat the bread and drink the cup each Lord's Day, we need to remember Christ's death in a very personal way. As I eat the bread, I need to remember that Jesus died for *me*. As I drink the cup, I need to remember that He had *me* in mind as His blood streamed from His body and puddled at the foot of the cross.

Also, as we participate in this memorial, Paul says "we pro-claim the Lord's death" (1 Corinthians 11:26). In other words, as we eat and drink, we're reenacting the event that brings salvation. It's a silent proclamation to everyone present that we really, truly believe Jesus's body was broken and His blood was shed for us, and for the sins of the entire world.

Future Hope

Not only do we "proclaim the Lord's death" as we eat the Supper, but we do so "until He comes" (1 Corinthians 11:26). That means we not only bring the past into the present when we eat, but we also proclaim our confidence in a glorious future.

You might say, then, that we're also bringing the future into the present as we eat. As we come to the table each Lord's Day, we're thinking about and rejoicing in our future inheritance that's guaranteed by the death and resurrection of Christ.

Covenant

In each recorded instance of Christ instituting His Supper, He spoke of His "blood of the covenant" (Matthew 26:28; Mark 14:24) or "the new covenant in My blood" (Luke 22:20; 1 Corinthians 11:25). This covenant language reminds us that we belong to the Lord, and this meal is reserved only for those who share the covenant.

The old covenant was inaugurated by sacrifice and the eating of a covenant meal (Exodus 24:3-11). For Christians, every time we eat the bread and drink the cup, we're renewing our covenant allegiance to the Lord. This simple weekly activity is a physical and visible expression that we are in covenant with God. It's a silent declaration that we belong exclusively to Him, and will remain exclusively loyal to Him.

Worthy Manner

Just before Paul tells us to "examine" ourselves, he speaks of eating and drinking "in an unworthy manner." He says, "Who-ever, therefore, eats the bread or drinks the cup of the Lord *in an unworthy manner* will be guilty concerning the body and blood of the Lord. *Let a person examine himself*, then, and so eat of the bread and drink of the cup" (1 Corinthians 11:27-28).

Focus on that word *manner.* Paul isn't talking about our wor-thiness to eat the Supper. As many have pointed out, none of us are, or ever will be, worthy to be a guest at Christ's table. He's talking about the attitudes and motives we bring to the table. He's telling us to do a thorough self-exam of our hearts as we prepare to partake because, contrary to what some may think, we don't earn points with God just by going through the right ritual at the right time.

Based on what we've just discussed about the meaning and significance of the Supper, I agree with those who say that four basic attitudes should fill our hearts when we meet with Christ and our fellow Christians at the table each Lord's Day.

To begin with, there should be *spiritual brokenness and con-fession*. If we honestly examine our hearts, we'll recognize how profoundly sinful we are and how desperately we need God's grace. There'll be a deep awareness of just how much we deserve hell, and a complete absence of spiritual pride.[16] This awareness will, in turn, lead to nothing less than a full confession of the sin that still infects us, as well as a confession that the sacrifice of Jesus is the only thing that will ultimately, and permanently, set us free from sin.

Another attitude that should be found at Christ's table is

reconciliation. As I've already pointed out, the Lord's Supper is a community activity. It's not just personal, private communion with the Lord. As we come to Supper, then, we'll come with a firm commitment to treat every one of our fellow partakers with the same respect, kindness, and concern. What's more, we'll come resolved to bend over backwards to try and heal any hurt that we may have inflicted, intentionally or unintentionally, on a brother or sister in Christ.

Still another attitude we should bring to the table is *rededication*. As we celebrate our intimate bond with Christ by eating the bread and drinking the cup, we renew our dedication and loyalty to Him. And part of that rededication is a reminder that true loyalty to Him will not allow us to form close associations with sinful things (1 Corinthians 10:21).

Finally, there should be *joy* in our hearts as we eat the Supper. As we eat the bread and drink the cup, we relive the events that guarantee our glorious future. And as we contemplate that future, we can't help but joyfully anticipate Jesus's return which will usher it in.

RESTORING THE SUPPER TO ITS RIGHTFUL PLACE AND TIME

So where does all this leave us? Well, for those of us who've been eating the Lord's Supper every Lord's Day for our entire Christian life, my prayer is two-pronged. First, I pray we'll remain passionately committed to that practice, fully convinced that it's God's plan and not just "our tradition." Second, I pray we'll never treat this profound—yet simple—weekly activity as just a superficial ritual that brings spiritual blessings and God's approval simply by going through the motions (that is, by partaking with little or no thought).

And for those of you who aren't presently following the New Testament pattern of observing the Lord's Supper each Sunday, I also have a two-pronged prayer for you. My prayer for you is that, one, you'll seriously think about what we've discussed in this chapter, and two, that you'll eventually celebrate the discovery of this important aspect of God's plan for His church and will want to unite with a group of believers who follow it.

CHAPTER 5

GENDER ROLES IN THE ASSEMBLY IN THE SHAPE OF THE NEW TESTAMENT

Every culture has its "do's" and "don'ts", and perched near the top of our culture's list of "don'ts" is any hint of discrimination on the basis of gender alone. If you want to see some real fireworks, just suggest that certain jobs should be off-limits to women just because they are women, then stand back and watch the show. Better yet, take cover or you just might be blown to bits. The point is, in our cultural corner of the world, the order of the day is that gender alone should never disqualify someone from doing what they want to do, and that includes doing what that they want to do in the life of their church. Here's part of a blog I recently stumbled upon which illustrates what I'm talking about:

> A few days ago, Rachel—my inquisitive 5 year old daughter—asked me an innocent question that she had been pondering over for some time and I have struggled with in times past.
>
> "Daddy," she asked, "Why are only boys preachers?"
>
> I agonize to myself at times over how to answer questions like this from my girls—mainly because my own personal views tend to not fall in line with the status quo in our church. I thought about it for a few moments, running through various scenarios in my mind, before I replied to

her with my sincere belief in the knowledge that my answer would most likely be contradictory to what she will hear in the Church of Christ.

"Honey," I said, "Some people think that God only wants that, but they are wrong. They are very wrong."

I'm betting you didn't miss the fact that this blogging dad claims membership in a church of Christ. Suddenly I feel compelled to remind you of something I told you way back on the second page of chapter 1. Do you remember when I said there are plenty of members of churches of Christ who won't be buying this book as a stocking stuffer for friends and family next Christmas? I'm going to make the bold prediction that this blogger is one of those members who won't be buying it and passing it around.

I'm also betting you didn't miss the fact that he admitted that his answer to his daughter's question "would most likely be contradictory to what she will hear in the Church of Christ." He's right about that. In most churches of Christ, when it comes to our church assemblies, the order of the day is male leadership.

What exactly does that look like? Well, when prayer is offered in our assemblies, only men lead it. And when God's Word is read to the assembled congregation, only men read it. And when someone preaches to the gathered church, that someone is always a man. And if there are any other individual speaking roles to be filled during our church assemblies, only men will fill those roles.

Although most church groups, at some point in their history, once shared this conviction, today more and more have distanced themselves from it. I'm not suggesting that churches of Christ are now all alone in this particular practice, but I am suggesting that it's rapidly disappearing from American church life. Several denominations and church groups still limit the role of preaching to men, but many—even a few churches that identify themselves as a "Church of Christ"—have opened up most other speaking roles in their worship assemblies to women (e.g., reading Scripture, leading singing, leading prayers, making announcements, etc.).

Of course most people in our culture would cheer the demise of what is, to them, an offensive, embarrassing relic of a bygone age of sexism and male-chauvinism. I can assure you, though, as far as I'm aware, there's not a sexist, chauvinistic bone in my body driving my commitment to this practice. In other words, this practice of ours is not one bit about male supremacy or superiority, at least not for most of us. Believe me, I've been outdone, out-played, out-thought, out-worked, and out-talked by too many women on too many occasions to think for a minute that I'm somehow intellectually, emotionally, spiritually or physically superior to women. As a man, do I think I'm different than women in many ways? Of course. Do I think I'm superior? Hardly.

If an out-of-date, sexist, chauvinistic mindset isn't driving our practice of male leadership in our assemblies, then what is? Actually, it's the same thing that drives all of our beliefs and practices, and that's an absolute commitment to conform as precisely as possible to the teaching of the New Testament.

Does the New Testament really teach what we practice? Obviously I'm convinced it does, but before I try to convince you, we need to take a quick look at the bigger picture of what the Bible says about men and women. If we don't start our discussion with that bigger picture, it would be easy for someone to wrongly conclude that we—and the Bible—are down on women.

EQUAL NATURES, EQUAL SALVATION, DIFFERENT ROLES

The very first chapter in the Bible begins its teaching about men and women by revealing that they are absolutely equal in nature. God made both in His image (Genesis 1:27). When He created the first couple, He didn't slip Adam an extra helping of His image. Both Adam and Eve possessed the fullness of God's image (whatever that is).

Scripture also teaches that men and women share equally in salvation (Galatians 3:26-27). Men don't receive salvation one way and women another. And men won't receive more of an eternal inheritance than women. Sorry guys, but we're not in line for any extra amenities in the new heaven and earth just because we're men. My wife is a "fellow heir of the grace of life" (1 Peter 3:7, NASB). In other words, she and I are in line for the exact same heavenly inheritance.

Finally, the Scriptures teach that husbands and wives are relationally equal. I don't possess my wife any more than she possesses me. Paul says we mutually possess each other: "The wife does not have authority over her own body, but the husband does; and likewise also the husband does not have authority over his own body, but the wife does" (1 Corinthians 7:4). For years my wife has worn a ring with a Hebrew inscription of our favorite verse from the Song of Songs, a verse that declares God's desire for husbands and wives to mutually possess one another: "I am my beloved's, and my beloved is mine" (Song of Songs 6:3).

Since my wife is my relational equal, the Bible doesn't command her to obey me in the same way it commands children to obey their parents (Ephesians 6:1), or employees to obey their employers (Ephesians 6:5). And since my wife is my relational equal, I better not treat her as if she were my child or my employee.

Despite the fact that men and women are absolute equals in both their nature and spiritual standing before God, and despite the fact that husbands and wives are relational equals, the second chapter in the Bible reveals that, from the beginning of creation, God wanted men and women to fill different roles and different functions in the home and in His spiritual community. The order in which God created Adam and Eve—Adam first, then Eve—wasn't meaningless happenstance. God did it that way on purpose for a reason.

According to the New Testament, when God created Adam first, that was His way of commissioning husbands to be leaders in the home, and men to be leaders in His church (1 Timothy 2:12-13; 1 Corinthians 11:3, 8-9). After creating Adam, God then created Eve for the specific purpose of being Adam's helper: "Then the Lord said, 'It is not good for the man to be alone; I will make him a helper suitable for him'" (Genesis 2:7, 18; see also 1 Corinthians 11:8-9). Although Eve was equal to Adam in nature, and was his relational equal as well, God intended for her to fill a supportive role as she and Adam carried out their God-ordained job description of filling the earth with His glory.

BIBLICAL HEADSHIP AND SUBMISSION

The New Testament uses the word "head" to describe the leadership role that God intends men to fill in both the home and church, and it uses the word "submit" to describe the support role that He intends women to fill in those settings. Notice, for instance, what Paul says to the Corinthians: "Now I want you to realize that the head of every man is Christ, and *the head of the woman is man*, and the head of Christ is God" (1 Corinthians 11:3). Similarly, he tells the Ephesians, "*wives, submit to your husbands* as to the Lord. For *the husband is the head of the wife* as Christ is the head of the church, his body, of which he is the Savior. Now as the church submits to Christ, so also *wives should submit to their husbands* in everything" (Ephesians 5:22-24). He also tells Titus to "teach the older women to . . . train the younger women to love their husbands and children, to be self-controlled and pure, to be busy at home, to be kind, and to *be subject to their husbands*, so that no one will malign the word of God" (Titus 2:3-5). Like Paul, Peter also instructs wives to "*be submissive to your husbands* so that, if any of them do not believe the word, they may be won over without words by the behavior of their wives" (1 Peter 3:1).

When most Americans hear those verses read out loud, it tends to have that fingernails-down-a-chalkboard effect on them. *Male headship. Female submission.* There's just something about the way those words ring in our modern American ears that makes us cringe. "Male headship" tends to conjure up offensive images like male domination, male privilege, and male superiority. And "female submission" sounds suspiciously like women should be powerless, voiceless, and essentially at the mercy of the whims and dictates of men.

Unfortunately, those offensive images have been actual reality throughout much of history, and far too many people have pointed to the Bible's call for male headship and female submission to justify it. Frankly, those who've done so are guilty of hijacking and perverting the biblical concepts of *headship* and *submission* to their own shame.

We need to take a minute or two to smash all unbiblical models of male headship and female submission by emphasizing what true biblical headship and submission really are . . . and what they're really not. Let's start with biblical headship.

Biblical headship simply means *Christ-like leadership*. Paul says "the husband is the head of the wife, **even as Christ is the head of the church**" (Ephesians 5:23). Male headship, in other words, is to be modeled after Christ's headship of the church. Then, right on the heels of saying that the husband is the head of the wife, Paul, in effect, looks every husband right in the eye, and says, "Husbands, **love your wives, just as Christ also loved the church and gave Himself up for her** . . . husbands ought to love their own wives as their own bodies. He who loves his own wife loves himself; for no one ever hated his own flesh, but nourishes and cherishes it, . . ." (Ephesians 5:25-29).

Since Jesus is the model of headship, clearly there's not an ounce of arrogance or a hint of dominance in biblical headship. Clearly biblical headship doesn't have the slightest resemblance to a self-absorbed dictator or a harsh, tyrannical monarch. And clearly it doesn't mean that, compared to women, men should feel superior, first-class, smarter, more important, more valuable, or more gifted.

Since Jesus models headship, it means caring for your wife as much as you care for yourself. It means cherishing, nourishing, and protecting her as you would yourself. It means longing to see her reach her fullest potential—spiritually, emotionally, physically, and intellectually—and it means you're willing to make personal sacrifices in order for that to happen. It means you're not going to ignore or minimize her wants, wishes, or feelings, and it means that her best interests will be at the very center of your heart.

Now what about biblical submission? Biblical submission simply means *Christ-like followership.* In 1 Corinthians 11:3 Paul says, "Christ is the head of every man, and the man is the head of a woman, and **God is the head of Christ**." Don't miss those last six words I highlighted—"God is the head of Christ." Just as Jesus is the model of headship, He's also the model of submission.

Nothing is clearer in Scripture than the fact that Jesus willingly submitted Himself to the Father's will and loving leadership (Matthew 26:19; John 4:34; 5:30; 6:38) despite the fact that He shares the same divine nature as the Father (John 1:1,14; 17:5; Philippians 2:5-6; Colossians 2:9).

Since Jesus is the model of submission, clearly there's not an ounce of weakness, not a drop of inferiority, and not a hint of a doormat mentality to be found in the biblical concept of submission. Clearly biblical submission doesn't mean second-class, enslaved, less important, powerless, or voiceless, and it says nothing about one's personal worth, talent, ability, or intelligence.

Since Jesus perfectly models submission in His relationship with the Father, female submission in the home simply means that a wife will acknowledge that God has commissioned her husband to be the primary leader in their home, and she will willingly allow him to fulfill that role. Similarly, female submission in the church simply means that Christian women will acknowledge that God has commissioned Christian men to be the primarily leaders in the church, and they will willingly allow godly men to fulfill that role.

REFLECTING GOD'S PLAN IN THE CHURCH

How exactly does our belief that only men should speak to the assembly fit into all this? To put it as concisely as I can, we believe God has called men alone to speak to the assembly to serve as a permanent, visual expression of His will for male headship and female submission among His people.

Recently I was reading a commentary by a well-known evangelical scholar who emphasized that the principle of male headship and female submission is an eternal principle that every congregation, in every culture, in every generation must acknowledge and reflect. At that point, I was with him all the way, and may have even written "amen" in the margin.

He then suggested that different cultures may *express* that principle in different ways, which means, among God's people, the *outward expressions* of the principle of male headship and female submission may differ from culture to culture.

Here's what it all boiled down to. He suggested that Paul's rules for women in church may have been a *first century* outward expression of the principle of female submission. And if that's true, we don't have to follow those rules if they don't culturally express the principle of female submission where we live. According to him, instead of adopting *first century* cultural expressions of female submission, we must adopt *our* cultural expressions of it. And that's where this evangelical scholar lost me.

Here's the problem with his proposal. Some cultures completely reject the principle of male headship and female submission, and where that principle is rejected, there are no cultural expressions of it. *News flash—twenty-first century American culture intensely rejects the principle of male headship and female submission, so we don't have any real cultural expressions of it.* Now what? How do God's people outwardly express male headship and female submission if they live in a culture that has no outward expressions of it?

Let me suggest that God, in His infinite knowledge, knew there would be cultures that would reject the principle of male headship and female submission. As a result, He not only commanded His people to acknowledge that principle, but He also instituted a couple of permanent, outward ways for them to express it, one of which is that women are not to speak to the gathered church.[1] Here's one place where the New Testament seems to clearly make this connection:

> As in all the churches of the saints, the women should keep
> silent in the churches. For they are not permitted to speak,
> but should be in submission, as the Law also says. If there is

anything they desire to learn, let them ask their husbands at home. For it is shameful for a woman to speak in church (1 Corinthians 14:33b-35).

These verses are actually part of a larger series of instructions where Paul establishes speaking-in-church rules for three groups. In addition to women, he also establishes rules for tongue speakers and prophets. Before we take a closer look at his rules for the women, let's take a look at his rules for these other two groups.

RULES FOR TONGUE SPEAKERS

The rules for tongue speakers are simple. Rule number one is a three speaker limit. Rule number two is they can only speak one at a time. And rule number three is each speaker must have an interpreter. If there's no interpreter for a tongue speaker, then that tongue speaker isn't allowed to speak to the assembled church. Here's how the Holy Spirit, speaking through Paul, puts it: "If any speak in a tongue, let there be only two or at most three, and each in turn, and let someone interpret. But if there is no one to interpret, let each of them keep silent in church and speak to himself and to God" (1 Corinthians 14:27-28).

The reason Paul won't let them speak without an interpreter is because no one in the assembly would know what's being said, except for God. That's why Paul tells tongue speakers to keep what they're saying between themselves and God when no one is present to interpret.

Paul's main point in this chapter is that everything done in church must be able to spiritually strengthen the congregation—or to use his words, "let all things be done for building up"

(1 Corinthians 14:26)—and the only thing that can accomplish that mission is a presentation of God's truth in understandable words. By the time Paul actually got around to banning non-interpreted tongues (1 Corinthians 14:28), he had already used quite a bit of ink explaining that, spiritually speaking, they have no nutritional value (1 Corinthians 14:1-25). Paul really says it all when he writes, "I would rather speak five words with my mind in order to instruct others, than ten thousand words in a tongue" (1 Corinthians 14:19).

RULES FOR PROPHETS

Paul's speaking-in-church rules for prophets are equally simple and basically the same as his rules for tongue speakers. There's a three speaker limit, and they can only speak one at a time. Here are those rules: "Let two or three prophets speak, and let the others weigh what is said. If a revelation is made to another sitting there, let the first be silent. For you can all prophesy one by one" (1 Corinthians 14:29-31a).

Paul then explains his reasoning behind these rules. First, they have to do it Paul's way "so that all may learn and all be encouraged" (1 Corinthians 14:31b). Nobody can learn anything through the verbal chaos that's created when people talk at the same time. Again, this is all about Paul's point that people can't be nourished spiritually unless they understand what's being said. Second, they have to do it Paul's way because "God is not a God of confusion but of peace" (1 Corinthians 14:33a). In other words, verbal chaos in the assembly not only violates God's will, but it violates His nature as well.

RULES FOR WOMEN

Paul's speaking-in-church rules for women appear to be just as simple and straightforward as his rules for tongue speakers and prophets. Rule number one is they are not permitted to speak . . . they are to keep silent. The end. There is no rule number two or three. Paul's exact words are: "As in all the churches of the saints, the women should keep silent in the churches. For they are not permitted to speak, but should be in submission, as the Law also says" (1 Corinthians 14:33b-34).

Now let's take a quick look at Paul's reasoning behind this rule. First of all, women are not to speak to the assembled church because that's the practice "in all the churches of the saints" (1 Corinthians 14:33b).[2] Some have suggested that Paul forbids women in Corinth from speaking in the church assembly only because it was offensive in Corinthian culture. His instructions don't apply, they say, in cultures where it's not offensive for women to speak publicly in church.

I don't think that line of reasoning takes seriously his words "as in all the churches of the saints." Those words seem to clearly show that culture has nothing to do with this rule. According to Paul, women weren't permitted to speak to the assembly in *any* church, in *any* place, in *any* culture. "As in all the churches of the saints" shows that Paul's instructions to the Corinthians were universal instructions. *Every* church, in *every* location, in *every* culture was expected to follow the same rules.

Paul's second reason for telling women not to speak in the church assembly is because they "should be in submission, as the Law also says" (1 Corinthians 14:34). This zeros in on the fundamental reason behind his rule. It shows that it has everything to do with God's permanent design of male headship and female submission.

When Paul refers simply to "the Law," he usually means "the Law of Moses" or the Old Testament Scriptures in general. By citing "the Law" in support of the principle of female submission, Paul seems to be saying that female submission has always been, and still is, a part of God's revealed plan for His people. His no-speaking-in-church rule, then, is to be understood as a permanent, universal, concrete expression of the principle of female submission among His people.

Paul gives a third reason for not allowing women to speak to the assembly when he says, "it is shameful for a woman to speak in church" (1 Corinthians 14:35). This could mean it's either shameful by the cultural standards of Corinth, or shameful from God's perspective. For arguments sake, let's assume Paul means that it's shameful from the perspective of Corinthian culture. That still doesn't mean his rule only applies where it's considered culturally shameful for a women to speak publicly in church. His rule still applies to *every* church in *every* culture because, as we just saw, his first two reasons for the rule have nothing to do with culture.

"BUT WHAT ABOUT . . ."

As people ponder Paul's words in 1 Corinthians 14:34-35, and ponder our straightforward understanding of them, some ask, *"What about women who are highly gifted Bible teachers?"* Our answer is, they should definitely exercise that gift . . . but not when the whole church assembles. There are other places in the life of the church where that gift can be used.

"What about women who are extraordinarily gifted public speakers?" Our answer is the same. They should definitely exercise that gift . . . but not when the whole church assembles. There are other places in the life of the church where women can, and should, use that gift.

"What about those women in New Testament times who had the gift of prophecy (Acts 2:17-18; 21:9; 1 Corinthians 11:5). They definitely exercised that gift, but Paul seems to make it very clear that they were not to exercise it when the whole church assembles. There were obviously other times and places where they used that gift.

"I OBJECT!"

Paul's speaking-in-church rules for women seem to be so straightforward that it's hard for me to imagine there could be any significant disagreement over what he means. But there is disagreement . . . and plenty of it. I should point out, though, that this hasn't always been the case. Historically, when Bible believers read, "women should keep silent in the churches," and "they are not permitted to speak," they understood it to mean that only men could speak to the gathered church.

Widespread disagreement over the meaning of what Paul said is a relatively recent development. And, quite frankly, I don't think it's a coincidence that these disagreements picked up speed about the same time that our culture was becoming indoctrinated in the belief that any hint of gender discrimination is an insidious evil.

Am I suggesting that the spirit of our culture is driving people to reject the most straightforward meaning of Paul's words? When you consider the timing of all this, I think it's almost impossible to avoid that conclusion. At any rate, let's take a look at some of the ways people try to explain how Paul's words don't really prohibit women from picking up a microphone and speaking in the church assembly.

Paul Didn't Say That

A few people actually insist that Paul didn't write 1 Corinthians 14:34-35. According to them, someone else must have added these two verses later, and that means we can just toss them out of the Bible. In other words, we can just ignore them. Problem solved.

That may sound like a great solution to some, but the fact is, virtually every New Testament scholar believes these verses are authentic. In other words, Paul really wrote them. So, while this "Paul-didn't-really-say-that" challenge is out there, it really isn't all that popular.

Miraculous, Not Non-Miraculous

Another way some people challenge the most straightforward meaning of Paul's words is to say he's only prohibiting miraculous, inspired speaking.

Here's how this argument goes. Since the first two types of speaking that Paul regulated were miraculous in nature—tongues and prophesy—then the type of speaking being done by the women in Corinth must have been miraculous too. Therefore, so the argument goes, Paul is only prohibiting women from doing miraculous, inspired speaking in church.

This interpretation has at least two gaping holes in it. First, are we really expected to believe that Paul was okay with *uninspired* women speaking to the church, but not okay with women who had a Holy Spirit-inspired message? If Paul didn't allow inspired women to speak to the assembly, then he surely didn't allow uninspired women to do so.

The second gaping hole is the fact that Paul doesn't even allow women to ask a question publicly when the whole church is assembled. If they have a question, he tells them to "ask their husbands at home" (1 Corinthians 14:35). Surely asking a question isn't miraculous speaking. Obviously, then, Paul isn't just prohibiting miraculous speech.

Wives, Not Women

Another attempt to make Paul's words more acceptable to modern readers is to say he's only talking to married women. According to this argument, since Paul tells the women to "ask their husbands at home" if they have a question (1 Corinthians 14:35), his speaking-in-church rules must be intended only for married women.

This attempt to avoid the most natural meaning of Paul's words doesn't stand up to scrutiny any better than the last one. Are we expected to believe that Paul is giving single ladies more freedom to speak to the church than married ones? Are we expected to believe God takes the microphone away from women in the church assembly the minute they say "I do"? If so, talk about your marriage penalties.

"If Paul means all women—married and unmarried—why does he specifically refer to their husbands"? There are a couple of possibilities. First, it's actually possible that Paul may be referring to more than just husbands. The Greek word translated "husbands" (*andres*) can also be translated "men," and refer to a woman's legal representative. In Greek society every woman had a "man" as her legal representative, and that "man" could be her father, brother, or uncle, as well as her husband. Paul may very well be using *andres* this way.[3]

I'm of the opinion, however, that Paul does mean "husbands," and he does so simply because he assumes most women in Corinth are married, just like most women in our culture are married, or have been married. If this is the case, then the principle is the same for both married and unmarried women—if they have questions, they should pursue answers outside of the assembly.

By the way, let me give you one more thing to think about. If Paul is only prohibiting married women from speaking publicly in the church assembly, does that really make it more acceptable to modern readers? I don't think so.

Correcting Some, Not Prohibiting All

Still another way some try to make this passage easier on our ears is to say Paul is correcting some *specific* speaking abuses that a *specific* group of women are committing. Here's a quick summary of this argument. Paul tells prophets who aren't speaking at the moment to "weigh" what the other prophets are saying (1 Corinthians 14:29). A few verses later, he tells the women to "ask their husbands at home" if they have any questions (1 Corinthians 14:35). The conclusion, then, is that Paul is talking specifically to *female prophets,* and he's telling them not to publicly question, or "weigh," the prophetic messages of their husbands (assuming, of course, their husbands are prophets). In other words, female prophets can prophesy in church; they just can't "weigh" the prophecies of their husbands in church.

I don't think this view stands up very well to close examination either. For one thing, it's difficult to understand why Paul would allow a female prophet to give a prophetic message to the church, but not allow her to give a prophetic examination of another prophet's message. For me, that idea struggles to pass the "common sense test."

Another problem with this view is that it takes some interpretive gymnastics to understand it that way. If that's what Paul really meant, then he said it in an incredibly awkward and confusing way. If you were to ask a thousand people who've never studied this passage to read it and explain what Paul means, I'm convinced that not a single person would say, "That's easy, he's telling female prophets that they can't 'weigh' their husbands' prophecies during church." When people say that, you can assume someone has helped them see it that way. That's definitely not a straightforward reading of Paul's words.

But there's an even bigger problem with this view. If Paul were simply correcting some specific speaking abuses of female prophets, then he would have told them when they could speak and when they couldn't. He wouldn't have told them to stop talking altogether.

How can I be so sure about that? Because that's what Paul did with both the tongue speakers and the prophets. He didn't stop them from speaking altogether in church. He just corrected their speaking abuses by telling them when they could and couldn't speak. But Paul doesn't do that with the women. When it comes to the women, he prohibits them from speaking altogether. In fact, as I've already pointed out, he even goes so far as to prohibit them from publicly asking questions in the assembly.

It's a Matter of Decorum

A fifth attempt to make this passage more palatable to modern taste buds goes something like this. Paul is talking specifically to *disruptive* women. He's calling down women who are having a hard time controlling their impulses to "pipe up" with questions in the assembly. The principle, however, applies to everyone, and that principle is that no one is to be disruptive in church. In other words, when Paul wrote this, he wasn't concerned about women speaking in the assembly; he was concerned about decorum in the assembly.

This is just another form of the argument that Paul is only correcting the speaking abuses of specific women. My primary objection to this view, then, is the same as my primary objection to the previous view—if Paul were just correcting certain speaking abuses by certain women, then he would have told them when they could speak and when they couldn't. But, again, he doesn't do that. Instead of telling the women when they can and can't speak, as he did with the tongue speakers and prophets, he prohibits them from speaking altogether in the assembly. He obviously has more in mind than decorum.

WHAT ABOUT 1 CORINTHIANS 11:5?

Perhaps the biggest reason that many evangelicals now reject a straightforward reading of this passage is because of something Paul says a little earlier in the same letter. Just three chapters earlier, he says, "every wife who prays or prophesies with her head uncovered dishonors her head" (1 Corinthians 11:5).

Many evangelicals assume this reference to women praying and prophesying indicates two things. One, they assume that women were leading prayers and prophesying in the church assembly at Corinth. Two, they assume that Paul approved of it.

Once these two things are *assumed*, they have to conclude that, three chapters later, Paul *can't* be saying women aren't allowed to speak in the assembly. That would be a contradiction, and Paul can't contradict himself. Their solution, then, is to reject the straightforward meaning of 1 Corinthians 14:34-35 and opt for a meaning which allows women to lead prayers and prophesy in church. In case you're wondering, the meaning which most evangelicals seem to opt for is the one where Paul is supposedly telling female prophets that they can't "weigh" their husbands' prophecies in the church assembly.

The major problem with this view lies in one of its two assumptions. I agree with their assumption that 1 Corinthians 11:5 indicates that women in Corinth were praying and prophesying in the church assembly.[4] The problem, in my opinion, is their second assumption—assuming that Paul approved of it. I'm convinced that this was one of several things going on in the church assembly at Corinth that he *didn't* approve of—like tongue speakers speaking without interpreters, multiple prophets speaking at the same time, and people turning the Lord's Supper into a potluck with a few close friends.

I'm convinced of this because elsewhere Paul gives very straightforward rules for church gatherings which seem to clearly prohibit women from leading prayer and prophesying.

First, of course, are his rules we've been talking about—1 Corinthians 14:34-35 —which, when read in a straightforward way, prohibit women from *any* public speaking role in the assembly.[5] Needless to say, this blanket prohibition would include leading prayer and prophesying.

Second, there are his equally straightforward rules in 1 Timothy 2 which also seem to clearly prohibit women from leading prayer and prophesying in church:

> *I desire then that in every place the men should pray,* lifting holy hands without anger or quarreling; likewise also that women should adorn themselves in respectable apparel, with modesty and self-control, not with braided hair and gold or pearls or costly attire, but with what is proper for women who profess godliness—with good works. Let a woman learn quietly with all submissiveness. *I do not permit a woman to teach or to exercise authority over a man;* rather, she is to remain quiet (1 Timothy 2:8-12).

Notice the first statement I highlighted—"I desire then that in every place the men should pray" (1 Timothy 2:8). There are two things to note here. First, when Paul says "the men," he uses a Greek word that specifically means "the males." He could have easily given this order without any gender specifics, but, under the supervision of the Holy Spirit, he specifically orders "the males" to pray. Second, the phrase "in every place" is essentially the equivalent of the phrase "in church" or "in assembly" in 1 Corinthians 14.[6]

By *specifically* ordering "the males" to pray in the assembly, Paul clearly excludes females from filling that role. In case you're wondering how that "clearly excludes females from filling that role," let me briefly summarize an important principle for interpreting Scripture—most of us in churches of Christ call it "the principle of silence"; others call it "the regulative principle."

When God *specifically* calls for certain things, He expects His people to understand that they aren't free to introduce something else. In Old Testament times, for example, when God *specifically* called for priests to come from the tribe of Levi (Numbers 3:5-13), the Israelites understood that they weren't free to select priests from any other tribe (Hebrews 7:14). Or when He *specifically* called for the ark of the covenant to be transported by the Levites in a certain way (Exodus 25:12-15; Numbers 4:5-6, 15), the Israelites understood that they weren't free to transport it any other way (1 Chronicles 15:1-2, 11-15).

This same principle is equally valid in New Testament times, and here are a few "for instances" to think about. Because Jesus instituted His Supper *specifically* with "bread" and "fruit of the vine" (Matthew 26:26-29), we understand that we aren't free to use Krispy Kremes and Gatorade instead. And when God *specifically* calls for people to be "immersed" in the name of the Jesus (Acts 2:38), we understand that we aren't free to sprinkle people instead. Or when He *specifically* calls for elders to be "the husband of one wife" (1 Timothy 3:2; Titus 1:5-6), we understand that we aren't free to appoint women to the eldership.

And that brings us to God's *specific* call for "the males" to pray when we gather for worship (1 Timothy 2:8). Because He *specifically* orders "the males" to pray in church settings, we understand that we aren't free to call on females to lead the congregation in prayer.

Now to the second statement I highlighted a minute ago in Paul's instructions to Timothy—"I do not permit a woman to teach...over a man" (1 Timothy 2:12). With these words, Paul prohibits women from *any* teaching in *any* church setting where men are present; and since prophesying was a means of instruction in the early church, this rule would have prohibited women from prophesying in the assembly.[7]

In both of these passages—1 Timothy 2:8-15 and 1 Corinthians 14:26-36—Paul's specific purpose is to govern speaking in the church assembly. Consequently, most of us in churches of Christ accept *these* rules as *the* rules for speaking in church. We don't believe anything can trump *these* rules. We believe everything must fit *these* rules. If something appears to contradict *these* rules—like an incidental reference to "every wife who prays or prophesies" in 1 Corinthians 11:5—we believe there must be a reasonable explanation which preserves *these* rules as Paul's final word on speaking in church.

Is there really a reasonable way to explain how Paul could

refer to women praying and prophesying in 1 Corinthians 11:5, and then turn around in 1 Corinthians 14:34-35 and say that women must not speak at all in the church assembly? I think there is a reasonable way to explain it, and I think it's found in how Paul deals with another issue in the same letter. That issue is whether a Christian can participate in a meal being served in an idol's temple. Let me walk you through it.

In the Roman world of New Testament times, paganism was the name of the game when it came to religion. Pagan temples dotted the landscape and played an important role not only in people's religious lives, but in their social lives as well. Dining rooms, or halls, were often physically attached to, or associated with, those temples, and they were commonly used for social occasions and cultural events.[8] As a result, it wouldn't have been unusual for believers in places like Corinth to be invited to dine at some of those temples by their pagan friends and associates. And, as you can probably imagine, the appropriateness of accepting such invitations became a matter of debate in the church there, and that debate prompted them to ask Paul for guidance.

In 1 Corinthians 8 Paul begins dealing with this matter. He starts out by agreeing in principle with the arguments made by those who think it's okay to eat in an idol's temple. By the end of the chapter, it looks like Paul also thinks it's okay, as long as a Christian's presence there "does not somehow become a stumbling block to the weak" (1 Corinthians 8:9).

But that's not Paul's last word on this matter. His last word comes two chapters later, in 1 Corinthians 10. There Paul's position on whether or not a Christian can eat in an idol's temple can be summed up in two words—*absolutely not!* He explains that idols may not be real, but demons are, and they are the driving force behind all idolatry. And that means eating in an idol's temple is actually communing with the demonic. His bottom line? "You cannot drink the cup of the Lord and the cup of demons. You cannot partake of the table of the Lord and the table of demons" (1 Corinthians 10:21).

Some might think Paul contradicted himself by answering this question one way in 1 Corinthians 8 and then giving a completely different answer in 1 Corinthians 10. But he didn't contradict himself. He just has a way of dealing with one issue at a time.

Here's what I mean. When Paul started exploring the question about eating in an idol's temple in 1 Corinthians 8, he chose to focus on the issue of Christian influence, and how our influence should always be a major consideration when we're confronted with choices. Then, when he gets to 1 Corinthians 10, he focuses on the reason why eating in an idol's temple is inherently wrong and therefore absolutely forbidden. Now can you see what I mean when I say that Paul sometimes deals with one issue at time when he writes?

Now let's move to the matter of women speaking in the assembly. I believe the reason Paul doesn't tell women to stop speaking in 1 Corinthians 11 is because he chooses to focus on a different issue at that moment—the issue of head coverings. He knew he was going to deal with the issue of women speaking a little later, so he chose not to deal with it in 1 Corinthians 11.

Again, it seems to be almost identical to how he handled the issue of eating in an idol's temple. He knew in 1 Corinthians 8 that the believers in Corinth shouldn't be eating in an idol's temple, but he chose to deal with something else at that moment, and he waited until 1 Corinthians 10 to tell them to stop. Similarly, in 1 Corinthians 11 Paul knew that women shouldn't be speaking in the assembly at Corinth, but he chose to deal with something else at that moment, and he waited until 1 Corinthians 14 to tell them to stop.

PAUL'S RULES OR GOD'S RULES?

Many people today dismiss Paul's speaking-in-church rules in 1 Corinthians 14 with a shrug of their shoulders and a statement, or a thought, like, "That's just Paul talking, not Jesus."

Actually it is Jesus talking. Paul is just Jesus's mouthpiece. After Paul finishes handing down his speaking-in-church rules, notice what he says: "If anyone thinks that he is a prophet, or spiritual, he should acknowledge that *the things I am writing to you are a command of the Lord*" (1 Corinthians 14:37). Let that statement sink in—"the things I am writing to you are a command of the Lord." To ignore or reject Paul's rules is to ignore or reject the Lord's rules.

Why did the Corinthian church need this reminder? I think the verse immediately before this one—which also happens to be the verse that comes immediately after his instructions to women—answers that question. In that verse, Paul poses these rhetorical questions to the Corinthians: "Or was it from you that the word of God came? Or are you the only ones it has reached?"

(1 Corinthians 14:36). If these questions sound a little bit like a rebuke, that's because they are a rebuke.

With these questions, Paul is rebuking a very dangerous spirit that apparently ran through the Corinthian church. They were acting as though they were the source of God's Word. They were acting as though they could decide what was right and what was wrong, and what was proper and what was improper. And they were acting as though they didn't have to obey the same rules that every other church had to obey.

It's to that independent spirit that Paul directs this rebuke and reminds them that he speaks with the authority of God. He spoke to that independent spirit when he told them, in effect, "You can't make your own rules, and you can't go your own way. The rules have been made by God, and you are to obey them just as every other church must obey them."

Paul's words here serve as an ongoing reminder to us today that God's church must never be shaped by our own desires or the spirit of our culture. Instead, it must be shaped by the Spirit of God who speaks through the words of His apostles (1 Thessalonians 1:13) which have been preserved in Scripture (2 Timothy 3:16-17).

RESTORING GOD'S PLAN FOR MEN AND WOMEN IN THE CHURCH ASSEMBLY

Despite the fact that more and more churches are distancing themselves from the historic Christian belief that God calls men alone to speak to the gathered church as an outward expression of His will for male headship and female submission, we remain as committed as ever to respecting that call. No matter how out of step with culture we may find ourselves for trying to precisely follow God's revealed plan for men and women in church, we're going to keep following that plan because His approval means more to us than our culture's. And if you see the importance of following that plan too, we hope you'll want to find a church home where you can live out that belief.

CHAPTER 6

CHURCH ORGANIZATION & LEADERSHIP IN THE SHAPE OF THE NEW TESTAMENT

"Are you the pastor?" Like most preachers, if I've been asked that question once, I've been asked it a thousand times. And then there are the occasional introductions I get—usually in non-church settings by folks who aren't members of a church of Christ—like, "This is Pastor Dan Chambers," or "He's the pastor of the church of Christ."

I'm fully aware that, in our culture, when people say "pastor," they basically mean "preacher" or "minister." And I know that people are just being courteous and respectful when they address me as "Pastor" or "Pastor Chambers." But for those of you who aren't very familiar with churches of Christ, I'm going to let you in on a little secret. The truth is, I'm always a teeny-tiny bit uncomfortable when someone addresses me that way, even though I don't show it because, like I said, I know they're just trying to be respectful.

Why the slight discomfort? Because in churches of Christ, preachers just aren't addressed as "Pastor" or "Pastor so and so." In fact, not only are they not *addressed* as "Pastor," they aren't even referred to as "a pastor" or "*the* pastor" of a church. Among our folks, preachers like me are usually just referred to as "a preacher" or "a minister." A few of my preacher friends prefer being called "an evangelist," but most of us are perfectly okay with being described as, and describing ourselves as, "the preacher" or "the minister" of a particular congregation. And in congregations that have a multi-staff ministry, the preacher's job title is usually "Pulpit Minister" since his primary *ministry* to the congregation is to stand in the *pulpit* and preach.

By the way, "pastor" isn't a designation we use for anyone on a ministry staff. That's right, we don't have "youth pastors" either. We have "youth *ministers*." If you check the website of the congregation I preach for, you'll see that we have three full-time ministers—a Pulpit Minister (that's me), a Youth Minister, and an Evangelism Minister.

So how do most of my fellow church members address me? Frankly, I've always requested they address me as "Right Reverend and Most Eminent Divine." Just kidding . . . but I did actually see a "clergyman" with that title several years ago. Seriously, though, everyone just calls me "Dan" (or "Danny" if they've known me for at least twenty-five years). There's also the occasional "brother Dan" or "brother Chambers" that I get, but most who call me "brother" usually call all of their fellow church members of the male persuasion "brother" as well.

By now some of you are probably thinking, "*What's the big deal? Do you really think calling a preacher 'the pastor' and addressing him as 'Pastor' are major issues?*" I'll admit that in the greater scheme of spiritual issues, someone calling me "Pastor" doesn't really get me too bent out shape. And when a non-member asks me, "Are you the pastor?" I've never really felt much of an urge to launch into an on-the-spot theological lecture to explain why I'm not (they didn't come to see me to be shown-up theologically). Instead, I usually just say "Yes," or something like, "Yes, I'm the preacher," so they can go ahead and get on with what's really on their mind.

With that being said, however, the reason we don't use the word "pastor" to describe preachers, youth ministers, or anyone else on a ministry staff is actually a small part of another big difference between churches of Christ and most other church groups. That difference is how the church is organized and governed. And we believe church organization and government is a big deal. Let me explain.

"WHO'S IN CHARGE AROUND HERE?"

I just grabbed my tattered old paperback copy of **Webster's New World Dictionary** and looked up the word "pastor." First it told me that it's the Latin word for "a shepherd." Then it gave this definition: "a clergyman in charge of a congregation." Both of those definitions zero in on the reasons we don't refer to the preacher as "the pastor." First, most preachers and other ministry staff in churches of Christ aren't "shepherds" in the true New Testament sense of the word. Second, the preacher is definitely not "in charge" in a church of Christ.

If not the preacher, who's in charge in a church of Christ? It's a group of men who meet several specific God-prescribed qualifications. Most of us usually call them "the elders," and the congregation I currently serve has seven elders who are collectively "in charge." While a few preachers in churches of Christ pull double-duty by also serving as an elder, the vast majority don't. I'm in that latter group—I'm not one of the elders of the congregation I preach for.

If you've been reading this book from the beginning, I'm sure you can guess the reason I'm about to give for why we're so committed to this kind of church leadership. It's because that's the pattern of church leadership in the New Testament. Throughout the New Testament, God gave the responsibility of leading and overseeing each local congregation to a plurality of men who met specific qualifications. Nowhere in the New Testament will you find a congregation that has just one "pastor" who is considered to be the leader of that church.

The Bible usually uses the term "elders" to identify the men who oversee a local congregation. In fact, the Greek word translated "elders" (*presbuteros*) is used at least fifteen times in the New Testament to refer to these church leaders. Here are a few of those occurrences: "And when they [Paul and Barnabas] had appointed *elders* for them in every church, with prayer and fasting they committed them to the Lord in whom they had believed" (Acts 14:23); "This is why I [Paul] left you [Titus] in Crete, so that you might put what remained into order, and appoint *elders* in every town as I directed you" (Titus 1:5); and "Is anyone among you sick? Let him call for *the elders* of the church, and let them pray over him . . ." (James 5:14).[1]

GETTING THE TERMS RIGHT

"If the Bible usually refers to the leaders of a congregation as 'elders,'

where does the term 'pastor' come from?" The term "pastor" is actually found in only one verse in most English translations of the New Testament. Here it is in the New American Standard (NASB) version: "And He gave some as apostles, and some as prophets, and some as evangelists, and ***some as pastors*** and teachers" (Ephesians 4:11).

The Greek word translated "pastors" in this verse is *poimen*, which actually means "a shepherd." In fact, *poimen* appears eighteen times in the Greek New Testament, and every time it appears—with the lone exception of Ephesians 4:11—it's translated "shepherd" in every major English translation. Don't ask me why most translations stick with the Latin word for "shepherd" in that one verse. I will tell you, though, that the English Standard Version (ESV), which came out in 2001, is the first major English translation to break with tradition and translate *poimen* as "shepherds" instead of "pastors" in Ephesians 4:11.

What Paul actually says in Ephesians 4:11, then, is that God placed "shepherds" in His church. The question is, "Who are these shepherds?" The answer, courtesy of both Paul and Peter, is that "shepherds" is just another way of referring to elders.

In the latter part of Acts 20, we find Paul in a place called Miletus, a port city on the southwestern coast of modern-day Turkey. While there, "he sent to Ephesus and called to him ***the elders*** of the church" (Acts 20:17).

In the inspired minutes of that meeting, Paul charged those elders to "be on guard for yourselves and for all the flock, among which the Holy Spirit has made you overseers, ***to shepherd the*** *church of God* which He purchased with His own blood" (Acts 20:28, NASB). "To shepherd" is a very literal translation of the Greek verb *poimaino*, which, as you can probably tell—even if you can't read any Greek—is the verb form of the noun *poimen* (shepherd). According to Paul, then, the Holy Spirit gave *elders* the responsibility *to shepherd* each congregation of God's people.

Peter backed up Paul's view that elders are the spiritual shepherds of God's people when he wrote: "I exhort **the elders** among you . . . **shepherd the flock of God** that is among you, exercising oversight, not under compulsion, but willingly, as God would have you; not for shameful gain, but eagerly" (1 Peter 5:1-2).

Since the word "shepherd" in the New Testament—or "pastor," if you're partial to the Latin form—refers to an elder, we in churches of Christ reserve the word "shepherd" for those who serve as elders. To call someone a shepherd who isn't an elder would be to use the term in a way that isn't biblically correct. I know that may sound like nit-picking to a lot of people, but our passion for trying to restore the beliefs and practices of the church in the New Testament makes us very sensitive to trying to use biblical terms as correctly as possible.

Let me add one more little caveat about the word "pastor." Since it's just another word for "shepherd," it would be just as biblically correct to call an elder "a pastor" as it would be to call him "a shepherd." With that said, however, it's highly unlikely you'll ever hear elders in a church of Christ referred to as "pastors." Why? Since the word "pastor" is now so entrenched in the larger Christian community to mean a minister—senior pastor, youth pastor, small-groups pastor, young adults pastor, worship pastor, etc.—it would cause a lot of confusion if we used it with a totally different meaning, even though that totally different meaning would be the biblically correct meaning. So, when we in churches of Christ refer to our elders, we generally stick to the words "elders" and "shepherds."

CHURCH ORGANIZATION: THE BIGGER PICTURE

Although there's more to be said about our commitment to following the New Testament pattern of having a plurality of elders govern each congregation, I think it's time to zoom out and talk about the New Testament pattern of church government from a wider perspective. After we do that, we'll zoom back in and talk some more about leadership in each local congregation.

Whether we're talking about a business, a government, a military, or a church, some form of organization and leadership will always be present because it's absolutely necessary. It's just a fact of life that group activities won't survive without some form of organization and leadership.

With that in mind, how should Jesus's church be organized and led? Has God left that decision to us? Has He given us the authority to implement what we think is the most effective and efficient form of organization and government? Or has God made that decision Himself?

I'm sure I've said enough in this chapter already, not to mention this whole book, that you know what we believe. When it comes to how the church should be organized and led, we're convinced that it's God's decision, not ours.

With that said, what kind of church organization and leadership has God revealed in the New Testament? As we make our way toward that answer, let's start by taking a quick look at the three basic types of church government that you'll find in the larger Christian community: *episcopal, presbyterian,* and *congregational.* The organization and government of every church group will fit into one of these three categories.

EPISCOPAL

An *episcopal* system of church organization and government gets its name from the Greek word *episkopos,* which is usually translated "overseer" in most English Bibles. In one New Testament passage—Philippians 1:1—a few versions, like the King James Version (KJV) and the New King James Version (NKJV), translate *episkopos* as "bishop."

Here are the places you'll find *episkopos* used in the New Testament: "Paul and Timothy, servants of Christ Jesus, To all the saints in Christ Jesus who are at Philippi, with **the overseers** and deacons" (Philippians 1:1); "Pay careful attention to yourselves and to all the flock, in which the Holy Spirit has made you **overseers** . . ." (Acts 20:28); "The saying is trustworthy: If anyone aspires to the office of **overseer,** he desires a noble task. Therefore **an overseer** must be . . . " (1 Timothy 3:1-2); and "For an **overseer,** as God's steward, must be above reproach . . ." (Titus 1:7).

In an episcopal system, a minister or priest typically has authority over a local congregation, but that congregation isn't independent or self-ruling. The authority over that congregation actually resides with someone who isn't one of its members, and that someone is usually called a "bishop." These bishops usually rule over a group of churches called a diocese. Some denominations with an episcopal system have an even higher level of authority whereby an "archbishop" rules over a group of bishops.

In this system of church government, the lower levels usually have little say in the selection of their leaders. Congregations usually have little or no say in the selection of the minister or priest who'll oversee them; ministers or priests have no say in the selection of the bishop who'll have authority over them; and bishops have no say in the selection of the archbishop to whom they'll report.

The most obvious example of a denomination with an episcopal form of government is the Roman Catholic Church. Trying to wrap your mind around all the details of how the Catholic Church is organized and governed can be quite the challenge. Generally speaking, though, the pope has ultimate authority and exercises direct authority over all the bishops, the bishops exercise authority over all the priests in a diocese, and a priest exercises authority in each local Catholic Church.

Eastern Orthodox Churches, the Anglican Church (that is, the Church of England), and the Episcopal Church—which is the American version of the Anglican Church—also have an episcopal form of organization and government which is very similar to the Roman Catholic Church, except they don't have a level of authority equal to the pope. Many Methodist churches, as well as some Lutheran churches, also have some form of an episcopal system of government.

PRESBYTERIAN

The second main type of church organization and government is *presbyterian*. This word comes from the Greek word *presbyteros*, which, as we've already seen, is usually translated "elder" in our English Bibles.

In a typical presbyterian system, each local congregation is governed by a group of elders, and these elders are selected by the congregation from among its own membership. But like an episcopal system, a presbyterian system also has another level of authority above the local congregation, which means congregations in a presbyterian system aren't independent or self-ruling either.

In a presbyterian system, all the churches in a particular geographic area select representatives to form a regional body of elders called a *presbytery*. That *presbytery*, then, governs all the congregations in its region. Among other things, this regional ruling body installs ministers in the churches under its care, disciplines ministers and congregations, organizes and dissolves congregations, and usually owns the property of each church in its region.

Most denominations which have a presbyterian system of government also have one or two levels of authority above the *presbytery*. Sometimes these higher levels are called *synods* and *general assemblies*. These higher levels typically oversee the national agencies of their denomination, propose doctrinal changes (which then must be ratified by the presbyteries), and function as courts of appeal concerning decisions made on lower levels.

I'll go ahead and state the obvious by telling you that all presbyterian denominations have a presbyterian system of government. Also, church groups which identify themselves as "Reformed" will, more often than not, have a presbyterian system of government.

CONGREGATIONAL

The third main form of church organization and government is called *congregational.* In a congregational system there is no level of authority above the local congregation. A word you'll often hear people use to describe this system is "autonomy," which simply means "self-rule." When you hear someone say, "we're autonomous," they're saying, "we're 100% independent and self-governing."

In a congregational system, no other church, no regional ruling body, and no denominational board or representative can tell a congregation what to do. Each church owns its own property, chooses its own leaders, selects its own ministers, and makes all of its own decisions.

Groups that have some form of a congregational system of government include Baptists, Congregationalists, independent Christian churches, and us—churches of Christ. Since the 1980s, one of the biggest trends in American church life has been for churches to cut their formal ties with denominations and start promoting themselves as "non-denominational" churches. Most of these churches also practice a congregational form of church government.

COMMITTED TO CONGREGATIONAL

As I just pointed out, we in churches of Christ embrace a congregational system of government. It's important to understand, though, that we don't embrace it because we discussed it and came to the conclusion that this system works best for us. We embrace it because that's the pattern found in the New Testament, and—I probably don't have to say it again, but I will—we're passionate about being a New Testament-shaped church.

As you read through the New Testament, you won't find a single reference to anyone who has authority over a local congregation except for the elders of that church and the apostles themselves. There's not the first reference to any kind of earthly headquarters that local churches must answer to, no mention of regional ruling bodies with authority over multiple churches, and no reference whatsoever to any kind of denominational organization to which local churches belong.

Here's something else which clearly shows that churches in the New Testament were autonomous. Most New Testament letters deal with problems, issues, and needs of particular local churches. When you read those letters, you'll notice that the apostles wrote directly to those churches, and to the individuals within those churches. They never wrote to anyone outside of those congregations who had authority over those congregations.

"What about Timothy and Titus? It sure looks like Timothy had authority over the church in Ephesus (1 Timothy 1:3), while Titus appears to have been in charge of all the churches on the island of Crete

(Titus 1:5)?" When you take a close look at Timothy and Titus, you'll see that they were trusted co-workers of the apostle Paul, and they served these churches as his personally commissioned representatives. These congregations recognized that these men had been personally sent to them by Paul with not only his instructions, but also his full apostolic authority.

As I said a moment ago, the only level of authority above the local congregation in the New Testament is the apostles themselves. They were handpicked by God to be His authoritative spokesmen among His people (Ephesians 3:4-5; 1 Thessalonians 2:13). The fact that God chose to speak through them is the reason they're called "the foundation" of His church (Ephesians 2:20). Their commands could not—and cannot—be contested by any congregation without incurring God's disapproval (1 Corinthians 14:37-38).

WHAT ABOUT ACTS 15?

Some people, however, actually claim that there is something like a regional ruling body in the New Testament. It's found, they say, in the book of Acts when Luke describes how the church at Antioch sent a group of its members to the Jerusalem church to get an answer to a question they were wrestling with (Acts 15:1-2). They wanted to know if circumcision was a necessary condition for salvation. In a nutshell, the answer that came back from Jerusalem was, "No, circumcision is not necessary for salvation."

At first glance, this may look like one church having authority over another. Or it may look like some kind of regional ruling body like a presbytery. If you look closely at this episode, however, you'll see that neither of those perceptions are reality.

The reason the Antioch church sent a group of its members to Jerusalem was because *that's where most of the apostles were.* Luke's exact words are that the Antioch church appointed a group "to go up to Jerusalem *to the apostles* and the elders about this question" (Acts 15:2). Then we're told: "When they came to Jerusalem, they were welcomed by the church and *the apostles* and the elders" (Acts 15:4). Next we learn that "*the apostles* and elders were gathered together to consider this matter" (Acts 15:6).

After deliberating and discussing the matter, "it seemed good to *the apostles* and the elders, with the whole church, to choose men from among them and send them to Antioch" with their answer (Acts 15:22). That answer was put in a letter, and that letter began, "The brothers, both *the apostles* and the elders, to the brothers who are of the Gentiles in Antioch and Syria and Cilicia" (Acts 15:23). Finally, we're told: "As they went on their way through the cities, they delivered . . . the decisions that had been reached by *the apostles* and elders who were in Jerusalem" (Acts 16:4).

I'm sure most of you noticed that Luke kept referring to the apostles and the Jerusalem elders together. Does this mean the Jerusalem elders had authority over the Antioch church? It doesn't mean that at all. One possible explanation for their close association in dealing with the Antioch-inquiry is that some of the apostles were probably part of the eldership of the Jerusalem church. After all, we know for sure that Peter was an elder (1 Peter 5:1), and there's good reason to think that he lived in Jerusalem at this time (Galatians 1:18). If that was the case, then it's easy to understand why this matter was decided by "the apostles and the elders." Of course, another real possibility is that the apostles, as members of the Jerusalem church, just felt it was important to involve the elders in the process of discussing and resolving this matter. At the end of the day, though, only the apostles had the authority to tell the Antioch church what to believe and do.

Today there is no church council or ruling body that's equivalent to the one in Acts 15 because, despite what some people think, there are no living apostles. With that said, though, the same apostles who had ultimate authority over every congregation in Acts 15 still have ultimate authority over every congregation today. In principle, then, what went on in Acts 15 should still be going on regularly in the Lord's church. When important questions pop up in a local congregation about what to believe and practice, the leadership of that congregation should consult with the apostles by carefully and thoroughly studying their writings which God has preserved in the New Testament.

TWO OFFICES IN THE LOCAL CHURCH

Now that we've seen that the New Testament pattern for church organization and government is clearly *congregational*, it's time to zoom in again and take a closer look at how each local congregation in the New Testament was organized and governed.

In the New Testament, God placed two special offices in the local church—*elder* and *deacon*—and there are a couple of passages which make this clear. First, there's Paul's letter to the church at Philippi which addresses "all the saints in Christ Jesus who are at Philippi, **with the overseers and deacons**" (Philippians 1:1). We'll see in a minute that the term "overseer" is used interchangeably with "elder"—for now, though, just take my word for it. The fact that Paul singled out "the overseers and deacons" from the rest of the church clearly shows that these were two distinct subgroups within the membership at Philippi.

Paul shows even more clearly that "elder" and "deacon" are special offices in the local church when he writes to Timothy and spells out the qualifications that a person must meet in order to serve in these two roles (1 Timothy 3:1-13). By the way, he also published a list of qualifications for elders when he wrote to Titus (Titus 1:5-9). The mere presence of additional qualifications to be an elder or deacon shows that these are distinct roles within the local church. Now let's take a closer look at these two special offices, and we'll start with the elders.

ELDERS

During Paul's first missionary journey, he and his co-worker Barnabas planted several churches in the southern tier of central Asia Minor (modern-day Turkey), and then "they appointed elders . . . in each church" (Acts 14:23). Similarly, Paul directed another co-worker, Titus, to "appoint elders in every town" on the island of Crete (Titus 1:5). Obviously, God's plan is for each congregation to have elders.

The New Testament uses three terms to describe this special role, and by now you shouldn't be a stranger to them—*presbyter* (elder), *episkopos* (overseer), and *poimen* (shepherd). We've already looked at the two passages which show that "elder" and "shepherd" are interchangeable, but now let me toss one of them back out so you can see that "overseer" is equally interchangeable with "elder" and "shepherd."

Let's go back to the city of Miletus where we find that Paul had "sent to Ephesus and called to him the **elders** (*presbyter*) of the church" (Acts 20:17, NASB). His apostolic orders to these men are: "Be on guard for yourselves and for all the flock, among which the Holy Spirit has made you **overseers** (*episkopos*), **to shepherd** (verb form of *poimen*) the church of God which He purchased with His own blood" (Acts 20:28, NASB). There you have it—they are *elders*, they are *overseers*, and they are *shepherds*.

Paul also used "overseer" and "elder" interchangeably when he told Titus: "This is why I left you in Crete, so that you might . . . **appoint elders** (*presbyter*) in every town as I directed you" (Titus 1:5). Then, among the qualifications that were to be used to screen potential elders, he told Titus: "**an overseer** (*episkopos*), as God's steward, must be above reproach" (Titus 1:7). Again, there you have it—an "overseer" and an "elder" are one and the same.

Now let me add a caveat about the word *episkopos*, like I did with the word "pastor" earlier. As I pointed out earlier, a few English translations render *episkopos* as "bishops" instead of "overseers" in Philippians 1:1. This means, of course, that "bishops" is just another way to refer to elders in the New Testament, and that means it would be perfectly biblical if we referred to our elders as "bishops." Nevertheless, you probably won't ever hear anyone in a church of Christ refer to their elders as "bishops" because that word carries a lot of undesirable baggage thanks to how some denominations have misused it to describe someone who's in charge of a group of congregations. So, again, most of us stick with the terms "elders" or "shepherds" when we refer to our elders (see what I mean).

THE WORK OF AN ELDER

The terms *elder, overseer,* and *shepherd* all combine to reveal that the primary work of elders is to direct the affairs of the local church and watch out for the spiritual well-being of each member.

The term "elder" (*presbyteros*) has a background in the Old Testament. In Old Testament times, families were led by the oldest, or "eldest," male. It was a system called "patriarchy," which means "rule by the fathers." In the New Testament, the church is God's spiritual family (Ephesians 2:19-20), and God's plan is for elders to function in the church as a father would function in a family. As the word "elder" implies, they are to be men of sufficient maturity and experience so they can effectively serve the family by being examples, administering discipline, dealing with disputes, setting responsible policies, and correctly interpreting and teaching God's Word.

The term "shepherd" (*poimen*), perhaps more than any other, helps us fully understand what the work of an elder is all about. Just as shepherds feed, protect, and take care of their sheep's injuries, the primary responsibility for feeding, protecting, and healing God's spiritual flock falls on the elders.

Elders must make sure that those under their care are being taught the truth of God's Word (i.e., sound doctrine) so they'll be able grow into spiritually mature image-bearers of Christ (Ephesians 4:11-16; Titus 1:9). That's feeding God's flock. They must also make sure that those under their care aren't exposed to false doctrine (Acts 20:28-30; Titus 1:9-11). That's protecting God's flock. And they must oversee the whole process of helping God's people deal with the on-going effects of sin in their lives (Ephesians 4:11-16). That's healing and taking care of the injuries that God's people are constantly sustaining in this fallen, sin-infected world.

Finally, there's the term "overseer" (*episkopos*). It's a term that literally means one who "watches over" or "looks after" someone or something. Long before New Testament times, it was a word used for different kinds of managers, foremen, supervisors, inspectors, and even tutors in an educational setting. By New Testament times, however, the meaning of *episkopos* had evolved a bit, but it still retained some sense of managing and directing a group's affairs.

This doesn't mean, however, that elders should see themselves primarily as "managers" of a congregation in the sense that we tend to think of a manager of a business. To see themselves primarily that way would be to ignore or minimize the attitudes and responsibilities that the Holy Spirit wants to convey with the terms "elder" and "shepherd."

Nor does having "overseers" mean that a congregation has no voice in its own affairs. While the church most certainly isn't a democracy, good overseers will always welcome, and genuinely consider, the input of the membership as they're trying to faithfully direct the affairs of the church. And on many important issues like selecting new elders and deacons, hiring ministry staff, and considering building programs, a good eldership intensely solicits input from the members.

THE QUALIFICATIONS OF AN ELDER

There are two more things that the New Testament teaches about elders that I need to point out. For one thing, they must meet certain qualifications. As I told you earlier, there are two places in the New Testament where the Holy Spirit gives us a list of qualifications for being an elder. You'll find one list in 1 Timothy 3:1-7 and the other in Titus 1:5-9. In churches of Christ, we take these qualifications so literally, and so seriously, that when we decide it's time to select elders, we almost always start the process with a careful and thorough church-wide study of both the work of an elder *and* these qualifications.

We don't believe that any qualification on these two lists can be waived when it comes time to select elders. Let me give you a for-instance. One of the qualifications found in both lists is that an elder must be "the husband of one wife" (1 Timothy 3:2; Titus 1:6). We believe, then, the eldership is restricted to married men whose marriage faithfully reflects God's plan of one man and one woman for life.

"*Must a Pastor Be Married? The New York Times Asks the Question.*" That was the title of a blog by Albert Mohler Jr., the president of The Southern Baptist Theological Seminary. It was actually a follow-up to comments which were attributed to him in a news story which appeared in *The New York Times* about "prejudice against single pastors."[2]

Mohler's answer to that question was that the Bible expects them to be married, but doesn't absolutely require it. He based his argument on Paul's instructions to Timothy and Titus that an overseer must be "the husband of one wife" (1 Timothy 3:2; Titus 1:6). According to Mohler, those passages "describe the pastor," and being the husband of one wife "clearly suggests that the minister will be married." But then he added, "The text does not explicitly state that a minister is not to be single." He ended his blog by asking his readers, "How would you answer it?"

My answer, which most people in churches of Christ would whole-heartedly endorse, would go something like this. It depends on what you mean by the word "pastor." If by "pastor" you mean a *preacher*—and obviously that's how both *The New York Times* and Dr. Mohler meant it—then the simple answer is, "No, a preacher doesn't have to be married."

"But what about those passages referenced by Mohler which say that an overseer must be 'the husband of one wife'"? The subject of both of those passages is "an overseer" (1 Timothy 3:2; Titus 1:7), which, as you know, is another word for elder in the New Testament. Of course, Paul also uses the word "elders" in the Titus passage (Titus 1:5). These passages, then, describe *elders*, not preachers.

Now back to the question, "Must a pastor be married?" Like I said, it depends on what you mean by the word "pastor." If you mean a preacher or minister, then the answer is, "No, a preacher doesn't have to be married." But if you're using "pastor" correctly to mean an elder, then our answer is, "Yes, an *elder* must be a married man."[3]

"But Mohler said that 1 Timothy 3:2 'does not explicitly state that

a minister is not to be single.'" First of all, again, this passage is about elders, not ministers. Second, there's more than one way to say that an elder *must* be married. Saying, "an elder is not to be single" is not the only way to say it. Here's another way you can say it: "an overseer **must be** . . . the husband of one wife" (1 Timothy 3:2). Frankly, I find it impossible to read those words and conclude that it's okay to appoint a bachelor to the eldership.

Before I leave this matter that "an overseer must be . . . the husband of one wife," let me mention one more way that some people attempt to make these words fit the view that bachelors can be elders. I first encountered it in graduate school, and it goes like this: "When Paul said that an elder must be 'the husband of one wife,' it seems he meant that an elder must be a man of sexual purity."

Frankly, I just can't buy that explanation. If that's what Paul meant, I can't imagine a more obscure way he could have said it. Paul often calls people to live sexually pure lives, and when he does, he's pretty straightforward. For instance, he tells the Thessalonians, "for this is the will of God . . . *that you abstain from sexual immorality*" (1 Thessalonians 4:3). Similarly, he tells the church at Corinth to "*flee from sexual immorality* . . ." (1 Corinthians 6:18). And to the Colossians, he writes: "**Put to death therefore what is earthly in you: sexual immorality**, impurity, passion, evil desire . . ." (Colossians 3:5).

If Paul intended to say that an elder must be sexually pure, I believe he would have chosen a different phrase than "an overseer must be . . . the husband of one wife." I find no compelling reason to reject the most natural, most straightforward meaning of those words. And the most natural, most straightforward meaning is that an elder *must be* married, and his marriage *must be* faithful to God's plan.

Another prerequisite for elders found in 1 Timothy 3 is that his children must be submissive or under control (1 Timothy 3:4), and on the list of qualifications in Titus, Paul even says that an elder must be a man whose "children are believers" (Titus 1:6). Therefore, we in churches of Christ also believe the eldership is restricted to men who have at least one child who is a Christian.

I know a few married men who would make wonderful shepherds, but, unfortunately, haven't been able to have children, and have chosen not to adopt. These godly men respect the Word of God so much that they gladly accept the fact that they'll never be able to serve the church as an elder. Instead of being bitter about what they can't do, though, you'll find them enthusiastically serving the church in many other ways with dedication and distinction.

The church belongs to God, and He knows what kind of leaders His people need if they are to become what He wants them to be. The qualifications of an elder were given by God to ensure that His flock receives the direction and spiritual care it needs. To ignore or minimize any of those qualifications is to ignore or minimize the very will of God for His church.

THE NUMBER OF ELDERS IN A CONGREGATION

The last thing I need to point out concerning elders is that churches in the New Testament always had more than one. You'll never see a congregation in the New Testament with just one elder overseeing it.

In Acts 14:23 we see Paul and Barnabas appoint *elders*—plural—in each church they planted. In Acts 15:2 a delegation from the church in Antioch goes to Jerusalem to see the apostles and the *elders*—plural—of the Jerusalem church. In Acts 20:17 Paul sent for the *elders*—plural—of the Ephesus church. In Philippians 1:1 Paul greets the *overseers*—plural—of the church at Philippi. In Titus 1:5 Paul tells Titus to appoint *elders*—plural—in every town (i.e., in every congregation. James says, in James 5:14, that if anyone is sick he should call the *elders*—plural—of the church. And in 1 Peter 5:1-2 Peter exhorts the *elders*—plural—among the congregations to whom he writes.

In each church of Christ in the New Testament, a plurality of elders who met certain qualifications exercised the spiritual authority in the congregation. We in churches of Christ today are totally committed to following that same New Testament pattern—every congregation in our fellowship that has elders will have a minimum of two.

DEACONS

Now let's think about deacons. The word "deacon" comes from the Greek word *diakonos*, and the general meaning of that word is "a servant, a helper, or someone who ministers to the needs of others."

This word *diakonos* is used two ways in the New Testament. Sometimes it's used in a general sense to refer to *any* Christian worker or servant. When it's used that way, it's usually translated "servant" (Romans 16:1; Colossians 1:7; 4:7; 1 Timothy 4:6).

Occasionally, however, the New Testament uses *diakonos* to refer to a group of men who meet certain qualifications, and who serve the church in some kind of special, or official, role. When it's used in this special sense, it's usually translated "deacon" (Philippians 1:1; 1 Timothy 3:8, 12).

THE QUALIFICATIONS OF A DEACON

As He did with elders, God has placed a list of qualifications in the New Testament that a person must meet in order to serve as a deacon. That list is found right on the heels of Paul's list of qualifications of an elder in 1 Timothy (1 Timothy 3:8-13). In most churches of Christ, when a congregation decides the time is right to appoint new deacons, they often begin the process the same way they begin the process of appointing elders—with public teaching on the work and qualifications of a deacon.

In churches of Christ we take the God-breathed qualifications of a deacon just as seriously as we take the God-breathed qualifications of an elder. For instance, just as Paul says that an elder must be "the husband of one wife," he also says, "let deacons each be the husband of one wife" (1 Timothy 3:12). Therefore, we believe the office of deacon, like the office of elder, is restricted only to married men whose marriage conforms to God's plan of one man and one woman for life.

Also, the Bible says that deacons, like elders, must manage "their children and their own households well" (1 Timothy 3:12). This means we also believe that the office of deacon is restricted to men who have children. It's important to point out, though, that the text doesn't say deacons must have children who believe. So, unlike elders, the office of deacon is open to men whose children have not yet reached an age when they've become Christians.

THE WORK OF A DEACON

The New Testament doesn't actually give us very much information on what deacons do, but a clue comes from the meaning of the word *diakonos*. As I mentioned a moment ago, the general meaning of that Greek word is "a servant, a helper, or a minister who serves the needs of others."

Deacons, then, are obviously devoted, trusted servants who tend to the many important details and tasks of a congregation's life. Although the seven men selected to take care of some widows in Acts 6:1-6 aren't actually called "deacons," they definitely could serve as a model for deacons. Not only were these men chosen by the church for a specific task, but they also had to meet certain qualifications to be chosen.

One other thing that needs to be mentioned about deacons is that, like every other member of a local church, they are under the oversight and authority of the elders. The elders "direct the affairs of the church" (1 Timothy 5:17, NIV), and the deacons are the trusted servants of the church who assist the elders in carrying out their work.

RESTORING THE ORGANIZATION
OF THE TRUE CHURCH

Because all Scripture is God-breathed (2 Timothy 3:16), we

believe God has spoken with regard to how He wants His church organized and governed. As a result, we don't believe we're free to rethink and replace the New Testament pattern of congregational self-rule with forms we might think are more efficient or better suited to our time and culture. Nor are we free to rethink and replace the New Testament pattern of local church leadership in which a plurality of elders govern each congregation and deacons assist the elders in carrying out their work. And finally, we don't believe we're free to ignore or minimize even one of the God-ordained qualifications for being an elder or deacon.

Unfortunately, when it comes to church organization and government, most church groups aren't fully conforming to the pattern found in the New Testament. Some are definitely closer than others, but most fall short to some degree. Our hope is that every Christian will come to see the importance of respecting God's plan for church organization, and will want to unite in a properly restored church structure.

CHAPTER 7

MYTHS & MISCONCEPTIONS ABOUT CHURCHES OF CHRIST

As with any church group, a quick Google search is the only thing standing between you and plenty of information, opinions, and answers to just about any question you may have about churches of Christ. Unfortunately, though, a lot of the stuff floating around in cyberspace doesn't do a very good job representing what most of us believe and how most of us think.

Let's face it, every church group has its haters out there—including some from its own ranks—and the internet is the perfect forum to caricaturize the object of their loathing. I thought it might be helpful, then, to address a few of the more common myths and misconceptions about churches of Christ that you may occasionally run into. By the way, most of these issues are related to some of the things I've already covered in the book, so if you have a couple of déjà vu moments and think you're reading something you've already read, it's probably because you'll occasionally be reading something you've already read.

MYTH 1—CHURCHES OF CHRIST BELIEVE THEY ARE THE ONLY ONES GOING TO HEAVEN

As I was growing up, from time to time I'd hear some version of this old joke: A minister dies and suddenly finds himself at the gates of heaven. Before settling in, Peter gives him the grand tour which included an introduction to those who were living in each room. At some point, Peter turns to the minister and whispers, "Shhhhh. I'll explain in a minute, but for now just be very quiet as we pass this next room." The minister follows Peter's lead and quietly tiptoes past the room. As he passes the room, he notices that, unlike the other rooms, this one doesn't have any windows and the door is completely shut. After putting some distance between themselves and that room, the minister asks Peter, "What was that all about? Why did we pass that room, and why did we have to be so quiet when we passed it?" And Peter replies, "That room is for members of the church of Christ. They think they're the only ones here, so we just don't bother them."

Actually that joke happens to be an equal opportunity joke. I once did an internet search and discovered that a bunch of religious groups have been on the receiving end of that punch line. Baptists, Catholics, Fundamentalists, Fundamentalist Protestants, born-again Christians, Christians in general, Evangelicals, United Methodists, Lutherans, Missouri Synod Lutherans, Muslims, Jehovah's Witnesses, and Mormons were just some of the groups which have also served as the subject of that joke.

I can honestly say that I've never actually heard a member of a church of Christ say we are the only ones going to heaven. I've heard plenty of people accuse us of believing and teaching that, but to the best of my recollection I haven't personally come face-to-face with it. With that said, however, I have no doubt you can find that belief among us. After all, since there are over

1.5 million adherents in almost 12,500 churches of Christ in the United States,[1] you can find almost any belief among us. I'm convinced, however, that the thinking of most of my brethren on this matter is a lot like mine, so let me tell you what I believe.

First, I don't believe people are automatically disqualified from heaven if the church they attend doesn't have the words "Church of Christ" nailed to the building or printed on the sign and stationary.

Second, I believe God saves everyone who meets His prescribed conditions for salvation. Let me remind you of the very first time He offered forgiveness in the name of Jesus. When people believed that Jesus was the crucified, resurrected Messiah, they asked Peter and the other apostles, "What shall we do?" (Acts 2:37). Peter's answer was, "Repent and be baptized every one of you in the name of Jesus Christ for the forgiveness of your sins, and you will receive the gift of the Holy Spirit" (Acts 2:38). Then we're told: "Those who received his word were baptized, and there were added that day about three thousand souls" (Acts 2:41).

Nothing has changed since that first Pentecost after Jesus's resurrection. Peter told the crowd that this promise was not only for them, but also "for your children and for all who are far off" (Acts 2:39). So, I believe with every ounce of my being that God forgives and gives His Spirit to everyone who believes Jesus is the Messiah, repents of their sins, and is immersed in the name of Jesus for the forgiveness of sins. Period.

"*What about someone who doesn't precisely follow Peter's instructions?*" While I gladly leave the ultimate status of their salvation to God, I have to confess that I'm genuinely concerned about their soul. And that means I'm going to try to persuade them to do the very same thing that the folks in Acts 2 were told to do, so they can be absolutely sure that they'll receive the very same blessings that the folks in Acts 2 received. If I can't persuade them to do that, I'll still be their friend and leave the matter of their salvation with God.

Third, I believe anyone who becomes a disciple of Jesus has an obligation to obey to the best of their knowledge and ability everything Jesus has commanded. I actually take what Jesus said to His apostles at face value: "Go therefore and make disciples of all nations, baptizing them in the name of the Father and of the Son and of the Holy Spirit, *teaching them to observe all that I have commanded you* . . ." (Matthew 28:19-20). I believe, then, that all immersed believers should see the importance of banding together in local congregations that conform to, and are committed to, every shred of the apostles' teaching (see Acts 2:42), including their teaching concerning the work, worship, and organization of the local church.

"What about those who are genuinely trying to obey God's will to the best of their knowledge and ability, but they've been the recipients of wrong information?" In other words, what about those who've been wrongly taught in certain areas? Do I think God's grace will cover errors in belief and practice that result from inaccurate teaching? I absolutely do believe that grace will cover some of our errors in understanding.

But I also believe two more things which are relevant to this question. One, I know there are limits to God's grace—go back and read Matthew 7:21-23 and you'll see what I mean— and I simply don't know what all those limits are. Two, I know *genuine* faith is not content to stay in disobedience once truth is discovered. With these things in mind, I'm going to do all I can to persuade others to see the importance of conforming to the New Testament pattern of living and church life. If I can't persuade them, though, I'll still respect them, be their friend, and leave the determination of their eternal status to God.

MYTH 2—CHURCHES OF CHRIST ARE A CULT

Anyone who knows what constitutes a genuine "cult" would never apply that label to churches of Christ. They may strongly disagree with some of our teaching, but they know we're not a cult.

So what is a cult? Josh McDowell and Don Stewart have extensively studied religious cults and point out that a cult is basically a group whose teaching deviates in major ways from the central doctrines of historic Christian faith.[2] They also point out that most cults share certain characteristics, such as:

- Believing God has revealed something special, or new, to them.[3]

- Having sources of authority in addition to the Bible.[4]

- Having a central human leader whom they view as a messenger of God with unique access to God.[5]

No one genuinely familiar with churches of Christ would ever claim that our foundational beliefs deviate from the central beliefs of historic Christianity. And anyone remotely familiar with churches of Christ knows that we believe the Bible is complete, sufficient, and not to be added to (2 Timothy 3:16-17; Jude 3; Revelation 22:18-19). Finally, anyone who really knows churches of Christ knows that we believe the original apostles are the only human leaders with authority over us. For these reasons, McDowell and Stewart don't identify and examine churches of Christ as a cult—nor does any other book on cults that I've ever seen.[6]

MYTH 3—CHURCHES OF CHRIST TEACH THAT A PERSON IS SAVED BY WORKS

No accusation against any church group could be more wrong than the accusation that churches of Christ believe a person is saved by works. Paul clearly told us that salvation is a "free gift" (Romans 6:23), which means it can't be worked for or earned. On top of that, he also specifically said our salvation "is not a result of works, so that no one may boast" (Ephesians 2:8-9), and "one is justified by faith apart from works of the law" (Romans 3:28).

As with any gift that someone may offer us, though, we have to accept God's gift of salvation. He intensely wants each of us to accept it (1 Timothy 2:4; 2 Peter 3:9), and He graciously tells us how to do that, but He's not going to force anyone to take it. It's our choice. We can take it or leave it. Take a look at this passage from the Old Testament book of Isaiah—it perfectly illustrates the fact that some gifts which God offers aren't accepted:

> I was ready to be sought by those who did not ask for me; I was ready to be found by those who did not seek me. I said, "Here I am, here I am," to a nation that was not called by my name. I spread out my hands all the day to a rebellious people, who walk in a way that is not good, following their own devices
> . . .

As Israel hurtled toward destruction because of their en-trenched spirit of rebellion, God pictures Himself standing in front of them, waving His arms, and yelling "Here I am! Here I am!" But His pleas fell on deaf ears, and the consequences would be tragic for Israel: "I will destine you for the sword . . . because, *when I called, you did not answer; when I spoke, you did not listen, but you did what was evil in my eyes and chose what I did not delight in*" (Isaiah 65:12).

God was able to spare Israel from their looming destruction. He wanted to spare them. He offered to spare them . . . no, make that, He begged them to let Him spare them. But the choice was theirs, and they chose not to accept God's offer.

How do we accept, or receive, God's offer to save us from our looming destruction? The short answer is, by faith, and that includes doing everything God commanded in order to be saved (see Acts 2:38 again). Perhaps it's this conviction of ours—that there are God-given conditions that must be met in order to receive salvation—that has led some people to charge us with believing in salvation by works instead of faith.

If that's the case, it's a terrible mistake to view our belief that we must obey God's gospel commands as an attempt to work, or earn, our way into heaven. It's a terrible mistake to put obeying God's gospel commands in the category of "works" which the New Testament clearly rules out as a way of salvation. When we obey God's gospel commands, it's not a work of merit . . . it's an act of faith. Back in chapter 2, in a section called "What About Faith?", I explained how faith and obedience are related.

You may want to flip back and take about two minutes to read that section again.

When we respond in obedience to God's gospel commands, we're not trying to work our way into heaven; we're just "obeying the gospel" (2 Thessalonians 1:8; 1 Peter 4:17), and we know we're not earning a thing. We're just, in effect, extending our hand to receive the gift of salvation that God is offering.

When the apostle Peter told the crowd on the Day of Pentecost to "Repent and be baptized, every one of you, in the name of Jesus for the forgiveness of your sins" (Acts 2:38), he wasn't telling them what to do to earn salvation. He was telling them what to do to receive it.

And when he "continued to exhort them, saying, 'save yourselves from this crooked generation'" (Acts 2:40), he wasn't saying that they could save themselves by their own works. He was simply saying that they had a choice of whether to accept God's offer to save them, and he was urging them to accept it.

And when "those who received his word were baptized" (Acts 2:41), they didn't think for a minute that they were earning their salvation. They were just, in faith, obeying the gospel.

Of course, some people may charge us with teaching a works-based system of salvation because, frankly, they may have actually heard a member of a church of Christ blurt out a cringe-worthy statement like this: "We are saved by works. James says Abraham was justified by works (James 2:21), and we're justified by works too (James 2:24)." Fortunately, I haven't heard that kind of statement very often among us, but, unfortunately, I have heard it a time or two in almost a quarter of a century of full-time ministry.

What makes a statement like that cringe-worthy is when it's said without any further explanation of what James obviously means. When you read his full discussion on "faith and works," he obviously means that a verbal profession of faith alone won't save anyone (James 2:14). Only genuine faith saves, and James makes it clear that genuine faith responds to God in obedience, like Abraham did (Hebrews 11:8, 17). In other words, James doesn't teach that Abraham was justified through his own works, but rather through a working (i.e., obedient) faith, and that's a huge difference. And he doesn't teach that we're justified through our own works either, but rather through the same kind of working (i.e., obedient) faith that Abraham had.

If you ever hear a member of a church of Christ imply that James taught a work-based system of salvation—which I pray you never do—you can rest assured that most of us totally reject that as a complete misrepresentation of what James taught. And if you ever hear someone say that the churches of Christ teach salvation by works, hopefully you'll kindly correct them.

MYTH 4—CHURCHES OF CHRIST BELIEVE IN BAPTISMAL REGENERATION

Another popular myth about churches of Christ is that we believe and teach a doctrine known as "baptismal regeneration." More than once I've been asked by evangelical friends, "Churches of Christ believe in baptismal regeneration, right?"

The answer to that question is, "Absolutely not." While we

do believe the New Testament teaches that baptism is a necessary condition for salvation, we totally reject the doctrine of "baptismal regeneration."

Many who accuse us of embracing this doctrine probably do so because they misunderstand what "baptismal regeneration" really is. They mistakenly believe it's just another way of describing the belief that baptism is necessary for salvation. In reality, though, it means a whole lot more than that.

"Baptismal regeneration" is the belief that *the physical act of baptism by itself* conveys God's saving grace to a sinner. Notice I emphasized the words "the physical act of baptism by itself." In other words, "baptismal regeneration" is the belief that anyone experiencing the physical act of baptism will be saved regardless of whether or not they have any personal faith in Christ, or even any knowledge of Christ.

The doctrine of "baptismal regeneration" is usually held by groups who baptize babies for the purpose of salvation. These groups believe all babies inherit the sins of Adam and Eve which must be removed in order to be saved; and they believe God will remove those inherited sins in baptism even though the infant has no knowledge of Christ or personal faith in Him.[7] Yes, as I said a moment ago, we believe that baptism is a God-appointed condition for salvation. But we completely reject the notion that there's any saving power in the physical act of baptism itself. Baptism is the time and place in which God promises to meet sinners in their faith, forgive their sins, and give them the Spirit (Mark 16:15-16; Acts 2:38; Acts 19:2-3; Acts 22:16; Colossians

2:11-12). When we're baptized into Christ (Romans 6:3-6; Galatians 3:26-27), we know it's the power of God working through our faith that saves us (Colossians 2:11-13), not the physical act of baptism.

Hopefully you remember our baptism discussion back in chapter 2. There I emphasized that the Bible clearly teaches that baptism has no spiritual value unless a person is first convinced that Jesus is the crucified and resurrected Son of God and then repents. If you don't remember, let me give you a really quick summary.

In Acts 2:38 Peter told the believing crowd to "Repent and be baptized . . . for the forgiveness of your sins." Repenting—changing their attitude toward sin—was just as necessary to receive forgiveness as being baptized. And Jesus Himself said, "Whoever believes and is baptized will be saved, but whoever does not believe will be condemned" (Mark 16:16). Believing that Jesus is the crucified and risen Savior is the very foundational condition for receiving salvation.

Many other passages also clearly show that baptism in the New Testament was always preceded by actions like listening to the gospel, believing Jesus is the risen Lord, repenting, and confessing faith in Christ (see Acts 8:12-13; Acts 16:14, 31, 34; 18:8; Romans 10:9-10; Colossians 2:12).

To sum it up, we definitely believe being immersed into Christ is the culminating God-appointed condition for receiving salvation, but we also definitely *don't* believe baptism is the only condition of salvation.

MYTH 5—CHURCHES OF CHRIST ARE LEGALISTIC CHURCHES

"Legalism" and "legalist" are words that are thrown around quite a bit these days, and in most church circles calling someone a legalist is about the meanest, nastiest thing you can say to a person. But even though it's thrown around a lot, I'm not sure most people properly understand what a legalist is. As I listen to the way it's used, I get the distinct impression that many people believe a legalist is someone who believes that it's really important to obey the full will of God. That's not what a legalist is though.

A legalist, properly understood, is someone who believes that the basis of salvation is law-keeping. In other words, he believes salvation is given or denied solely on the basis of how well a person keeps God's laws. If you ask a legalist why he expects to receive eternal life, he'll say, "Because I kept the law of God," instead of, "Because Jesus paid for all my sins on the cross." Actually, he probably wouldn't say that, but in the deepest part of his heart he would believe it.

Although I can only speak for myself, I'm convinced that most members in churches of Christ know that God's gracious, unmerited gift of Jesus on the cross is the "because" of their salvation. In other words, I'm convinced that most of us know we're saved *because* God put all our sins on Jesus and then poured out on Him every ounce of His holy wrath that our sins deserve. We know that no matter how perfectly we keep God's commands, we're still sinners who deserve to go to hell, and so every single day we throw ourselves on the finished work of Jesus Christ in full trusting faith that His work is our only hope.

But that's not the only thing we do every single day. We also try to be fully obedient to God every single day. As I've said throughout this book, we're convinced we have an obligation as God's people to obey His will as fully and precisely as we possibly can.

We believe obedience is the sum total of all that God has asked us to do, which reminds me of the Old Testament story of King Saul and his unwillingness to fully obey God. Maybe you remember how God told Saul to completely wipe out the Amalekites—men, women, children, oxen, sheep, camels, donkeys. Nothing was to be left alive (1 Samuel 15:3).

When Saul got those orders, he didn't waste any time. He mustered the troops, marched them to the city of Amalek, and proceeded to wipe them out . . . but. But he did leave one man alive—the Amalekite king—and he spared the best of the livestock. God then responded to Saul's disobedience by dispatching the prophet Samuel to pay him a little visit. The minute Samuel showed up, you get the real sense Saul knew why Samuel was there because the first thing he said to Samuel was, "I have performed the commandment of the Lord" (1 Samuel 15:13). Samuel, in effect, responded with, "Really? Hmmm, my hearing must be playing tricks on me because I hear a lot of sheep and cattle with distinct Amalekite accents."

Even though the jig was obviously up, Saul still hoped that Samuel would buy this one last-ditch excuse: "Oh, yea, about that . . . we spared those so we could sacrifice them to God, but everything else we killed." And that's when Samuel uttered those famous and incredibly important words: "To obey is better than sacrifice" (1 Samuel 15:22).

Make no mistake about it, God has put obedience at the top of His list. If someone were to ask me to come up with just one word to describe what it means to *love* Christ, I would have to say "obedience." After all, Jesus said, "Whoever has my commandments and keeps them, he it is who loves me" (John 14:21).

And if I had to come up with one word to describe what it means to really *know* Jesus, once again I'd have to say "obedience." After all, John said, "By this we know that we have come to know him, if we keep his commandments. Whoever says 'I know him' but does not keep his commandments is a liar, and the truth is not in him" (1 John 2:3-4).

And if someone said, "Dan, give me just one word to describe what it means to call Jesus your Lord," I wouldn't have to think twice. I'd say "obedience." After all, Jesus said, "Why do you call me 'Lord, Lord,' and not do what I tell you?" (Luke 6:46).

Unfortunately, I believe with all my heart that the primary problem we've seen in American church life over the last thirty years or so—including in many churches of Christ—is a loss of commitment to total, sold-out obedience to God in everything. The type of Christianity being marketed for the last several years in our culture requires very little, if any, commitment to fully obeying God's Word. Among church leaders today, there seems to be a strong commitment to give churchgoers an intoxicating emotional experience, and a strong commitment to cultivate in them a spirit of service. But, sadly, there seems to be little commitment to teaching churchgoers how important it is to obey God's Word as precisely as possible in every circumstance and setting.

I'm aware that an "all in" approach to obedience is out of step with much of the current thinking among professing Christians, but we're absolutely committed to it. We're committed to obeying God whether other people obey or not. We're committed to obeying Him whether we like what He says or not. We're committed to obeying Him whether it makes sense to us or not. We're committed to obeying Him even if it means we have to go our separate ways from some of our closest friends and family. We're committed to obeying Him even if it means we'll be laughed at and portrayed in unflattering ways because of our commitment. Bottom line—we're committed to obeying God no matter what.

Now let me quickly explain how obedience fits into the issue of our salvation. In one of the most familiar passages in the New Testament, Paul said we're saved "*by* grace . . . *through* faith . . . *for* good works" (Ephesians 2:8-10). Those words make it crystal clear that our works aren't the cause of our salvation. Grace is the cause; we are saved "*by* grace." But Paul makes it equally clear that true saving faith *results* in a life of good works (i.e., obedience). In other words, where real faith exists, a life of obedience to God will also exist. On the other hand, if there's no obedience, there's no real faith. That's what James meant when he said, "faith by itself, if it does not have works, is dead . . . I will show you my faith by my works" (James 2:18).

If you're ever in a hospital room when someone dies, you'll see the medical staff check the body for signs of life. They'll

CHURCHES IN THE SHAPE OF SCRIPTURE

listen for a heartbeat, search for a pulse, and check the pupils of the eyes. They know if life is still in that body, signs of life will still be present. In the same way, if there's true saving faith in a person, signs of faith will be present. Obedience to God is the sign that genuine faith is present.

Again, let me emphasize that our passionate commitment to be fully obedient to God's will doesn't earn us salvation. If we thought it did, that would be legalism. We're committed to living in full obedience to God because that's what people of genuine faith do.

MYTH 6—CHURCHES OF CHRIST TREAT WOMEN AS SECOND-CLASS CITIZENS

Paul told the church in Galatia: "For in Christ Jesus you are all sons of God, through faith. For as many of you as were baptized into Christ have put on Christ. There is neither Jew nor Greek, there is neither slave nor free, there is no male and female, for you are all one in Christ Jesus. And if you are Christ's, then you are Abraham's offspring, heirs according to promise" (Galatians 3:26-29).

The point of this passage is that all people, men *and* women, have equal access to Christ, and all who belong to Christ, men *and* women, will share equally in the salvation God offers in Christ. As I said back in chapter 5, men don't receive salvation one way and women another. Both men and women "put on Christ" when "through faith" they are "baptized into Christ." And when that happens, they both become "heirs according to promise."

Another passage which shows that men and women have

equal spiritual standing before God comes from Peter. In his first letter he orders husbands to show honor to their wives "since they are heirs with you of the grace of life" (1 Peter 3:7). Make no mistake about it, men and women will *equally* share the future blessings of salvation. We in churches of Christ believe that with all of our hearts.

Not only do we believe men and women have equal access to equal spiritual blessings, but as I also pointed out in chapter 5, we believe men and women are equal in nature, and husbands and wives are relationally equal.

As far as church life goes, just as women played very prominent, very important, very central roles in church life during New Testament times,[8] they play very prominent, very important, very central roles in churches of Christ today. And just as they garnered respect, public recognition, and praise from the apostles themselves for their active and prominent involvement in church life during Bible times (e.g., Acts 9:36; Romans 16:2, 6), women today garner respect, public recognition, and praise from appreciative congregations everywhere for their active and prominent involvement in the life of the church.

It's true, of course, that most churches of Christ believe that a few roles in church life are reserved for men as an outward expression of God's plan for male spiritual leadership in His church. But that general belief isn't unique to us. Some form of that belief is shared by most conservative church groups because the most natural, most straightforward reading of several New Testament passages restrict a few roles in church life to men (1 Timothy 2:8-15; 3:1-2,12; 1 Corinthians 14:33b-35).

Some suggest that believing in male leadership in church life means believing men are superior, smarter, more important, more valuable, or more gifted than women. But that's simply not true. We don't believe that for a millisecond. And some suggest that wherever male leadership in church life is found, women are repressed, unappreciated, and treated as second-class citizens. Nothing could be further from the truth. If you were to randomly poll women in churches of Christ and ask, "Do you feel repressed, unappreciated, and like a second-class citizen in your church?", and if you guarantee their answer will remain completely anonymous, I'm convinced there would be hundreds of "no's" for every "yes."

Of course, no matter what I say or how I say it, I realize many in our culture will never back off their charge that we treat women as second-class citizens until we open every role in church life to men and women alike. Frankly, since most of us in churches of Christ are committed to being shaped by Scripture rather than culture, that day will never come—much to the chagrin of our critics. I suppose all we can really do, then, is to carefully and thoroughly teach Biblical manhood and womanhood with kindness and humility, and then just take the inevitable criticism in stride.

MYTH 7—CHURCHES OF CHRIST ARE A DENOMINATION

We live in a three dimensional physical world—a world of length, width, and height. Naturally, then, our minds can't conceive of another dimension. Similarly, we essentially live in a three dimensional Christian world—a world of Catholic, Protestant, and Orthodox—and so our minds have a difficult time conceiving of any other dimension of Christianity.

For those who profess to be Christians, the world asks, "Catholic, Protestant, or Orthodox?" And if the answer is "Protestant," the next question is "Which denomination?" Even churches which claim to be "non-denominational" tend to be thought of as a single denominational grouping within the Protestant tradition of Christianity.

We believe, however, there's another dimension of Christianity, and our goal is to serve Christ in that other dimension. In order to set this other dimension apart from the three dimensions of Catholic-Protestant-Orthodox, most of us call it "New Testament Christianity."

The true church of Jesus Christ in the New Testament was pre-Catholic, pre-Protestant, and pre-Orthodox. It was pre-denominational. The fact of the matter is, you won't find the first mention of any denomination in the New Testament. What you'll find is that followers of Christ considered themselves simply to be members of the church which He built and which belongs to Him (Matthew 16:18). And what you'll find is that Jesus's church was a loose network of independent, local congregations which conformed to the same general pattern of beliefs and practices. That, of course, is what we're trying to be. As I've said repeatedly in this book, our goal is to restore the true church of Jesus Christ by restoring the beliefs and practices of the church in the New Testament. We just want to be New Testament-shaped churches.

In her book *The Unauthorized Guide to Choosing a Church*, Carmen Renee Berry rightly says that churches of Christ "have no central headquarters with no overriding organizational structure—at all."[9] She goes on to say, "I respect the way they have translated their beliefs into action. They believe the original church was organized around local congregations. Other groups agree with this idea but go right ahead and organize denominations anyway."[10] She then contends that churches of Christ are "more consistent in living out their beliefs, in my opinion, than any other in this regard."[11]

In the back of her book, you'll find a list of thirty-five church groups with their official website. "Churches of Christ" is the only one of those thirty-five groups with "no web site."[12] And in her chapter on churches of Christ, she mentions how, in spite of no formal organization, they've done things like create several colleges and establish homes for abandoned children and the elderly. She then notes, "Not bad for a group that can't be called up on the phone."[13] Why can't churches of Christ "be called up on the phone"? Because churches of Christ aren't part of an actual denomination. There is no denomination called "The Church of Christ." Again, we're just a loose network of independent, local churches which conform to a similar package of beliefs and practices.

Of course, I'll be the first to admit that it's not easy to be *un*denominational in a denominational world. Even plenty of folks in churches of Christ just can't seem to break out of a denominational mindset; they still believe they're members of a denomination called "The Church of Christ."

You can usually spot those who think this way because they

tend to use the designation "church of Christ" as a denominational label. For instance, they may refer to a "Church-of-Christ preacher" or a "Church-of-Christ school" or even—and nothing makes me cringe more than this one—a "Church-of-Christ Church." And when asked, "What are you religiously?" they'll usually respond, "I'm Church of Christ," or some will just say— much to my horror—"I'm C-O-C."

And as much as I hate to admit it, there's also plenty who claim membership in a church of Christ who have completely given up the quest to restore *un*denominational New Testament Christianity. They insist it's time we admit that we're just one valid denomination among many and joyfully embrace that concept.

Although it's really hard to be *un*denominational in a denominational world, and although a few members have waved the white flag and given up the quest to return to Christian beginnings, most of us still embrace that vision. Most of us haven't surrendered . . . and don't plan to. So, we still try very hard to avoid using "church of Christ" as a denominational label. I don't know if you picked up on it or not, but throughout this book I've referred to our *fellowship* (not "our denomination") as "churches of Christ," not "*the* Church of Christ."

The point is, most of us still try very hard to use "church of Christ" the way Paul used it when he told the church in Rome, "all the churches of Christ greet you" (Romans 16:16). When he said that, he wasn't referring to a denomination called "The Church of Christ." He was simply referring to every congregation that belongs to Christ.

And that's what we're trying to be. We're just trying to be congregations that belong to Christ; congregations committed to restoring the beliefs and practices of the church in the New Testament; congregations trying very hard to return to Christian beginnings.

As I said in chapter 1, among the membership of most churches of Christ you'll discover that many are former members of various denominational church groups. Both of my parents and my wife's parents fall into that category.

When they came to see the importance of conforming to God's revealed pattern for His church, and when they learned that dividing people into different denominations wasn't part of that pattern, they decided to live out those beliefs. They were determined to make whatever changes were necessary in order to more fully conform to the same simple pattern that every church in the New Testament was expected to follow. In churches of Christ they sure didn't find perfection, but they did find that same determination.

If the idea of restoring the true church of Jesus Christ also appeals to you—that is, if you also see the importance of being part of a church that tries to conform to the same general pattern of beliefs and practices that churches in the New Testament were expected to follow—I hope you'll call a church of Christ in your area and ask for some more information. Or if you'd prefer, shoot me an email at danleola@yahoo.com; I'd love to send some resources your way or just answer any more questions you may have about what we in churches of Christ are trying to be and do as Jesus's followers.

ENDNOTES

CHAPTER 1

1. The Feast of Tabernacles is also known as the Feast of Booths (Leviticus 23:34). These booths were intended to remind the Israelites of the temporary structures they lived in as they wandered in the wilderness during the exodus from Egypt (Leviticus 23:39-43).

2. Corinth was in modern-day Greece while the region of Galatia was in the central part of modern-day Turkey.

3. Troas was on the northwestern coast of modern Turkey.

4. The Greek word translated "men" in 1 Timothy 2:8 is *aner*, which specifically means "a male person." In other places, even in this same chapter, Paul speaks of "men" in the general sense of "mankind" or "all people" (1 Timothy 2:2,4,5 in the NASB or the NKJV). When Paul means "men" in this general sense, he uses the Greek word *anthropos*, which means "a human being."

5. Everett Ferguson, "*Topos* in 1 Timothy 2:8," *Restoration Quarterly* 33 (1991): 65-73. Tom Schreiner cites Ferguson's article when he says, "When Paul calls on men to pray 'in every place' . . . this is probably a reference to house churches. Thus the directives here relate to a public church meeting when believers are gathered together. The words 'in every place' refer to all churches everywhere . . ." (Thomas R. Schreiner, "An Interpretation of 1 Timothy 2:9-15" in *Women in the Church: An Analysis and Application of 1 Timothy 2:9-15*, eds. Andreas J. Kostenberger and Thomas R. Shreiner, 2nd ed. (Grand Rapids: Baker Academic, 2005), 91).

6. Carmen Renee Berry, *The Unauthorized Guide to Choosing a Church* (Grand Rapids: Brazos Press, 2003), 238.

7. Ibid., 239.

8. Ibid.

9. Ibid., 348.

10. Ibid., 238-239.

CHAPTER 2

1. Huldreich Zwingli, "Of Baptism," in *Zwingli and Bullinger*, "Library of Christian Classics," vol. 24, ed. and trans. by G.W. Bromiley (Philadelphia: Westminster Press, 1953), 130.

2. Ibid., 156. "The doctors" were theologians, and "the Fathers" were the influential Christian teachers and writers who lived from roughly A.D. 100 to A.D. 500.

3. In all fairness to those "doctors" and "Fathers," Zwingli's charge that they all believed "the water itself effects cleansing and salvation" is just not true. Most, if not all of them, believed it was the blood of Christ that cleanses and saves; they just believed that God saves people through that blood at the moment of Christian baptism. Please don't think, however, that I'm giving "the doctors" and "the Fathers" a free pass concerning everything they thought and taught about baptism. I too believe that a lot of them got a lot of things wrong about baptism. For instance, replacing immersion with sprinkling, and doing away with belief and repentance as prerequisites for baptism, are two things that many of them got terribly wrong. I'll have more to say about these things later in this chapter.

4. "Epilogue" in *Women in the Church: An Analysis and Application of 1 Timothy 2:9-15*, 2d ed., eds. Andreas J. Kostenberger and Thomas R. Schreiner (Grand Rapids: Baker Academic, 2005), 175.

5. For a very thorough and very well documented discussion of Zwingli's understanding of baptism I strongly recommend Jack Cottrell, "Baptism According to the Reformed Tradition" in *Baptism and the Remission of Sins: An Historical Perspective*, ed. David W. Fletcher (Joplin, MO: College Press, 1990), 39-81.

6. As Neil Lightfoot says, in the case of these verses "the evidence apparently looks in two directions" (Neil Lightfoot, *How We Got The Bible*, 3rd Edition (Grand Rapids: Baker, 2003), 101). In other words, there's very strong evidence to both support and reject the authenticity of these verses. If you're interested in exploring the question of whether or not Mark 16:9-20 was an original part of Mark's gospel, I'd recommend *Perspectives on the Ending of Mark: Four Views*, ed. David Alan Black (Nashville: B&H Academic, 2008).

7. The Greek word translated "believes" in John 3:16 (*pisteuo*) is a verb form of the Greek word translated "faith" in Romans 5:1 (*pistis*). Our English translations use the word "believes" in John 3:16 simply because we don't have a verb form of the word "faith" in English. Since we can't say "whoever faiths in him should not perish," we have to say "whoever believes in him should not perish." In the New Testament, then, being saved through "faith" in Jesus is exactly the same thing as being saved by "believing in" Him.

8. It's hard to escape the conclusion that the main culprit behind this misunderstanding of faith is the fact that we use the English word "believes" in places like John 3:16. Since our word "believes" basically means "to accept something as true or real," it's easy to see how people would read that meaning into John's thinking.

9. Acts 11:14 (the conversion of Cornelius' household); Acts 16:15 (the conversion of Lydia's household); Acts 16:33 (the conversion of the Philippian jailer's household); Acts 18:8 (the conversion of Crispus' household).

10. Jack Cottrell, *The Faith Once For All: Bible Doctrine For Today* (Joplin, MO: College Press, 2002), 373.

CHAPTER 3

1. James McKinnon, *The Temple, the Church Fathers and Early Western Chant* (Brookfield: Ashgate Publishing Company, 1998), 69.

2. For a more thorough summary of the Church Fathers' rejection of instruments in worship, I highly recommend John Price, *Old Light On New Worship: Musical Instruments and the Worship of God, a Theological, Historical and Psychological Study* (Avinger, TX: Simpson Publishing, 2005), 71-83.

3. Robert Godfrey, *Pleasing God in Our Worship* (Wheaton, IL: Crossway Books, 1999), 40.

4. There's actually one recorded instance of an organ being used in worship prior to the 800s, and that was when Pope Vitalianus introduced an organ into a church in Rome about the year 670 (Philip Schaff, *History of the Christian Church* (New York: Charles Scribner's Sons, 1910: reprint ed., Vol. 4, Grand Rapids: Eerdmans, 1985), 439).

5. Joseph Bingham, *The Antiquities of the Christian Church*, 2nd ed. (London: Simpkin, Marshall, and Co., 1870), Vol. 1, 315.

6. John McClintock and James Strong, *Cyclopedia of Biblical, Theological and Ecclesiastical Literature* (New York: Harper & Brothers Publishers, 1879), Vol, 8, 739.

7. Quoted in Nick Needham, "Worship Through the Ages" in *Give Praise to God: A Vision for Reforming Worship: Celebrating the Legacy of James Montgomery Boice* (Phillipsburg, NJ: P & R Publishing, 2003), 393.

8. Timothy George, *Theology of the Reformers* (Nashville, TN: Broadman & Holman Publishers, 1988), 131. The "Great Minster" was the church in Zurich, Switzerland which served as the home base for Zwingli's reforming work.

9. John Calvin, *Commentary Upon the Book of Psalms*, vol. 1 (Grand Rapids: Eerdmans, 1949), 539.

10. Ibid.

11. Price, 109-110.

12. Ibid.

13. Henry Wilder Foote, *Three Centuries of American Hymnody* (Cambridge, MA: Harvard University Press, 1940), 86.

14. Horton Davies, *The Worship of the American Puritans* (New York: Peter Lang Publishing, Inc., 1990; reprint, New York: Soli Deo Gloria Publications, 1999), 126.

15. Ibid., 145.

16. John Spencer Curwen, *Studies in Worship Music* (London: J. Curwen & Sons, 1890), 179.

17. George, 131.

18. David Benedict, *Fifty Years Among the Baptists* (New York: Sheldon & Company, 1860), 283.

19. John MacArthur, Jr., *Ashamed of the Gospel: When the Church Becomes Like the World* (Wheaton, IL: Crossway Books, 1993), xviii.

20. Charles H. Spurgeon, *The Treasury of David*, vol. 2 (New York: Funk & Wagnalls, 1885), 301.

21. F. LaGard Smith, *The Cultural Church* (Nashville: 21st Century Christian, 1992), 199.

22. Godfrey, 40.

23. John Price, *Old Light On New Worship: Musical Instruments and the Worship of God, a Theological, Historical and Psychological Study* (Avinger, TX: Simpson Publishing, 2005), 71-83.

24. Ibid., 12.

25. Ibid., 16.

CHAPTER 4

1. "A British Baptist Speaks," an interview of George R. Beasley-Murray by John A. Owston in *One Body* (Spring 1991): 16.

2. If you're not familiar with "Calvinism," suffice it to say that it's a theological system that begins with a particular view of God's sovereignty (that is, how God exercises His rule over all things) and leads to conclusions about human freedom and salvation that I don't believe the Bible teaches. If you're interested in learning more about Calvinism, and exploring a fair critique of its problems, I'd recommend Jerry L. Walls and Joseph R. Dongell, *Why I Am Not a Calvinist* (Downers Grove, IL: IVP Books, 2004), and F. LaGard Smith, *Troubling Questions for Calvinists . . . And All the Rest of Us* (Nashville: Cotswold Publishing, 2007).

3. "First day of the week" was a Jewish designation. Jews customarily numbered the first five days in the week which led up to the day of Preparation (Friday) and the Sabbath (the seventh day, Saturday). What they called the "first day of the week," then, was what we call Sunday.

4. Justin Martyr, *Apology*, 1.67, quoted in Everett Ferguson, *Early Christians Speak*, rev. ed. (Abilene: ACU Press, 1987), 67.

5. "Didache" means "teaching," and the first line of this document reads, "Teaching of the Lord to the Gentiles by the twelve apostles."

6. Didache 14:1, quoted in Ferguson, *Early Christians Speak*, 67. There's plenty of evidence to show that the expression "the Lord's Day" came to be used very early among Christians to refer to the first day of the week, or Sunday. John, for instance, says he received his apocalyptic revelation from Christ "on the Lord's Day" (Revelation 1:10).

7. Paul's warning about not "discerning the body" is often applied to Christ's physical body, but the context clearly shows that the body Paul has in mind is Christ's spiritual body, the church.

8. The "president" is the one who "presides." This, then, is simply a reference to the person who leads the church in worship.

9. Justin Martyr, *Apology*, 1.67, quoted in Everett Ferguson, *Early Christians Speak*, rev. ed. (Abilene: ACU Press, 1987), 81-82.

10. If any further confirmation is really necessary to be sure that Justin is talking about the Lord's Supper, earlier in his letter he refers to this "bread and a cup of wine mixed with water" as "the Eucharist"—Eucharist, of course, being one way that many refer to the Lord's Supper (*Apology*, 1.65-66).

11. Didache 14:1, quoted in Ferguson, *Early Christians Speak*, 67.

12. John identifies the specific day that Jesus appeared to His apostles in John 20:26 as "eight days later." Scholars agree that the way the Jews counted days, John was referring to the next "first day of the week."

13. F. LaGard Smith, *Radical Restoration: A Call for Pure and Simple Christianity* (Cotswold Publishing, 2001), 139.

14. Ibid., 139-140.

15. Some argue that observing the Lord's Supper on Saturday is a Biblical practice because, they say, the service in Acts 20:7 was held on what would be our Saturday evening (in Jewish culture each new day begins at sundown, so in Jewish culture the "first day of the week" begins on our Saturday evening). In response to this argument, first of all, we can't be absolutely certain if the Troas church followed Jewish time (days begin at sundown), Roman time (days begin at midnight), or Greek time (days begin at sunrise). The fact is, however, that it doesn't really matter how the Troas church measured time. Whatever way they measured time, it was "the first day of the week" in their culture. When it comes to observing the Lord's Supper today, people should follow the time of whatever culture they're in. In American culture, Saturday night is not the first day of the week.

16. To see the difference between spiritual brokenness and spiritual pride, read the parable of the Pharisee and tax collector in Luke 18:9-14.

CHAPTER 5

1. The other permanent, outward expression of the principle of male headship and female submission is that women are not to exercise authority over a man (1 Timothy 2:12). This outward expression of male headship is seen most clearly in God's call for men alone to serve as elders and deacons in each church (1 Timothy 3:1-2, 12).

2. It seems best to join the expression "as in all the churches of the saints" (1 Corinthians 14:33b) with 1 Corinthians 14:34, and that's what most translations do. Some of those translations are the New International Version (NIV), the English Standard Version (ESV), the Revised Standard Version (RSV), the New Revised Standard Version (NRSV), the American Standard Version (ASV), the New Century Version (NCV), the Holman Christian Standard Bible (HCSB), the Amplified Bible (AMP), the Contemporary English Version (CEV), the GOD'S WORD Translation (GW), and the Good News Translation (GNT).

3. Everett Ferguson, *Women in the Church* (Chickasha, Oklahoma: Yeoman Press, 2003), 18.

4. Some suggest that the setting of 1 Corinthians 11:5 is not a church assembly. They acknowledge that it's some sort of a public setting, but say it can't be a meeting of the whole church since Paul forbids women to speak in the assembly in chapter 14. A main support for this argument is Acts 21:8-12 which describes the prophet Agabus speaking to a group in a public setting that was not a church assembly. This shows, they say, that there were public settings when prophets spoke which were not church gatherings. While this suggestion can't be completely ruled out, I think the most natural reading of 1 Corinthians 11:1ff suggests that a church assembly is being described.

5. This doesn't mean that women are prohibited from all forms of speaking in the assembly. It means they're prohibited from individually speaking to the church. Some speaking in church is done by the whole congregation together, and women are to participate in these group-speaking activities. Examples would be congregational singing (Ephesians 5:18-20), the congregational "amen" following congregational prayers (1 Corinthians 14:6), and a congregational prayer or reading of a Bible text. Also, since confessing faith in Christ "with the mouth" is a God-ordained condition of salvation (Romans 10:10), if a woman chooses to be baptized into Christ during an assembly of the church, naturally she would be expected to make that confession "with the mouth" to the congregation. Since all Christians are authorized to "confess your sins to one another" (James 5:16), I've heard of some cultures where both men and women verbally confess their sins in the assembly. These would be legitimate exceptions to the rule that women should not individually speak to the assembly.

6. Everett Ferguson, "*Topos* in 1 Timothy 2:8," *Restoration Quarterly* 33 (1991): 65-73.

7. Since many evangelicals believe 1 Corinthians 11:5 authorizes women to prophesy in the assembly, but at the same time believe 1 Timothy 2:12 prohibits them from preaching or teaching in the assembly, they must find a way to explain how prophesying in church is a completely different animal than preaching or teaching in church. Frankly, I haven't found their arguments to be very convincing. Generally speaking, the Bible indicates that both prophesying and preaching were actions through which a message from God was delivered verbally to the congregation. The difference between the two was simply that a prophetic message was directly inspired by the Holy Spirit. I'm convinced that biblical preaching in the church assembly today looks very much like—and functions essentially the same as—prophesying in the earliest church assemblies.

8. Leon Morris, *1 Corinthians* in the Tyndale New Testament Commentaries, rev. ed. (Grand Rapids: Eerdmans, 1990), 125-127; Richard Oster, *1 Corinthians* in The College Press NIV Commentary (Joplin, MO: College Press, 1995), 198-199.

CHAPTER 6

1. The other places where "elders" (*presybuteros*) are mentioned in the New Testament are Acts 11:29-30; 15:2, 4, 6, 22, 23; 16:4; 20:17; 21:18; 1 Timothy 4:14; 5:17; and 1 Peter 5:1.

2. http://www.albertmohler.com/2011/03/25/must-a-pastor-be-married-the-new-york-times-asks-the-question/

3. This doesn't mean I believe an elder who has been faithfully married for half a century, and who has faithfully helped to shepherd a congregation of God's people for three consecutive decades, must immediately step down from the eldership if his wife suddenly dies. It seems that God commanded elders to be married because He knew that certain qualities which are necessary for effectively shepherding His people can only be developed and demonstrated in the context of faithful marriage and parenting. In a case like the one I just described, most of us believe the widowed elder developed and demonstrated those qualities over a lifetime of marriage, and those qualities still qualify him to serve as a shepherd.

CHAPTER 7

1. *Churches of Christ in the United States*, 2012 edition (Nashville: 21st Century Christian, 2012), 20.

2. Josh McDowell and Don Stewart, *Understanding the Cults* (San Bernadino, CA: Here's Life Publishers, 1982). McDowell and Stewart identify and examine the following cultic religious groups: Hare Krishna, Jehovah's Witnesses, Mormonism, Transcendental Meditation, Theosophy, EST, Children of God, The Unification Church ("Moonies"), The Way International, The Worldwide Church of God, Christian Science, and Unity.

3. The Mormons (or the Church of Jesus Christ of Latter-day Saints, or simply LDS), for instance, teach that God revealed new "truth" to Joseph Smith, the founder of the Mormonism. That new revelation to Smith was published in 1830 as *The Book of Mormon*.

4. These other sources of authority may be other written works or they

may be a leader whose interpretation of the Bible is considered to be the final authority. An example of this is also found in Mormonism. In addition to the Bible, the Mormons have three other written works which they consider to be sacred and authoritative: *The Book of Mormon, The Pearl of Great Price,* and *Doctrines and Covenants.* And just listen to what their founder, Joseph Smith, said about *The Book of Mormon:* "The Book of Mormon is the most correct of any book on earth and the keystone of our religion." He also said that "a man would get nearer to God by abiding by its precepts, than by any other book." These quotes came from an official LDS website (jospehsmith.net).

5. The Mormons, again, illustrate what I'm talking about. According to an official LDS website (mormon.org), they believe "Jesus Christ began to restore His church in its fullness to the earth through the Prophet Joseph Smith in 1820." Here is another quote about Joseph Smith from an official website of the Mormon Church (jospehsmith.net): "Joseph Smith's first vision stands today as the greatest event in world history since the birth, ministry, and resurrection of Jesus Christ. After centuries of darkness, the Lord opened the heavens to reveal His word and restore His church through His chosen prophet." The current President of the Mormon Church, who is also given the title of a "prophet, seer, and revelator" of God's will on earth, is Thomas Monson.

6. Other books on cults that I checked were H. Wayne House, *Charts of Cults, Sects, and Religious Movements* (Zondervan, 2000), and Ron Rhodes, *The Challenge of the Cults and New Religions* (Zondervan, 2001).

7. Roman Catholics and Lutherans are two denominations that baptize babies for salvation (of course, they actually sprinkle or pour water on them, but they call it baptism). Other denominations baptize babies as well, but not for salvation. These other denominations, like Presbyterians and Methodists, view baptism as the New Testament equivalent to the Old Testament practice of circumcision. In the Old Testament, circumcision was an outward sign that a person belonged to God's Old Covenant community. So, denominations like Presbyterians and Methodists baptize babies basically as a sign they belong to God's New Covenant community, the church.

I feel it's important to remind you that nowhere in the New Testament is baptism described as a sign that a person belongs to the church, or that it's the New Testament equivalent of Old Testament circumcision. The only place where the New Testament makes a connection between baptism and circumcision is in Colossians 2:11-12, and there baptism isn't depicted as the New Testament equivalent of Old Testament circumcision. In that passage the apostle Paul simply uses the image of circumcision to describe what happens to a person "in baptism." Just as a person's physical flesh is actually removed in the operation of circumcision, so a person's spiritual flesh—that is, their sins— is actually removed "in baptism, in which you were also raised up with Him through faith in the working of God" (Colossians 2:12).

8. In the New Testament some women prophesied (Acts 2:17-18; Acts 21:9, 1 Corinthians 11:5), some were involved in teaching (Acts 18:24-25; Titus 2:3-5), some were recognized for their work in advancing the gospel (Philippians 4:2-3), some were recognized for their work in the local church (Romans 16:2,3,6,12), some hosted the church in their homes (Acts 16:15,40), some provided financial support for Jesus and His disciples (Luke 8:1-3), some were well known for their many good works and acts of charity (Acts 9:36), and some seem to have been engaged in some type of compensated service on behalf of the church (1 Timothy 5:9-12).

9. Carmen Renee Berry, *The Unauthorized Guide to Choosing a Church* (Grand Rapids: Brazos Press, 2003), 238.

10. Ibid., 239.

11. Ibid.

12. Ibid., 348.

13. Ibid., 238-239.

CPSIA information can be obtained
at www.ICGtesting.com
Printed in the USA
FFOW04n1426180916
27640FF